DESTINATION
Success

Editors:
Melissa Thomas • Melinda Miley • Michelle Groves Futrell

Kendall Hunt
publishing company

The Arthur Ravenel Bridge is an eight-lane, cable-stayed bridge that extends 2.5 miles over the Cooper River in Charleston, South Carolina. The bridge, which opened in 2005, was named after Charleston politician Arthur Ravenel who led the construction campaign. The bridge features two diamond-shaped towers that allow clearance for freighters to access Charleston's Port. The bridge has a bike and pedestrian lane and is the highlight of the annual Cooper River Bridge Run, the third largest 10K event in the United States.

Arthur Ravenel Bridge photo: Cover photo courtesy of Melinda Miley.

Road map image © 2015, Shutterstock, Inc.

Clip art illustrations used for icons © 2015, Shutterstock, Inc.

www.kendallhunt.com
Send all inquiries to:
4050 Westmark Drive
Dubuque, IA 52004-1840

CONTENTS

CHAPTER 8: DESTINATION: HEALTHY SUCCESS 205

Michelle Futrell

CHAPTER 9: PATH FORWARD 231

Mindy Miley

CHAPTER 1

CHECKING THE ENGINE: A REALITY CHECK

By Shannon Farrelly

1. LEARNING OUTCOMES: QUESTIONS TO NAVIGATE
   a. What is your current academic situation?
   b. What led you to this current situation?
   c. Where are you going and how will you get there?

2. KEY CONCEPTS
   a. Academic standing
   b. GPA
   c. Satisfactory academic progress
   d. Critical reflection
   e. Storytelling
   f. Professor Relationships
   g. Email etiquette

INTRODUCTION

This book provides you with a road map on your journey to academic success. You define your academic success. It's not your parent's definition, your academic advisor's definition, or your friends' definition. Everyone's image of academic success will differ. Your definition may focus on completion of your degree, admission to graduate school, a specific GPA, or becoming a life-long learner. However you define your academic success, there are some fundamental places along your academic journey that must be mastered and personalized for you to make academic success a reality.

Consider this chapter to be the beginning of your journey. Each subsequent chapter may require your attention for more or less time depending on what you need for your journey. Whenever you begin a road trip, there are several items to consider before hopping in the car. You must consider where you want to go by asking yourself where you want to end up. This location is where you picture yourself being happy and confident in your choices. Your definition of academic success is where you should imagine this road trip ending. You may not know what this looks like yet or how to get there, but that is what this book will help you define.

In planning a road trip, you must consider where you have visited. Your past experiences, people you have met, and the habits you have formed all influence where you are today. These important aspects also influence where you want to go, whether you want to return to any of those places, or if you want to try new experiences on the way to your destination. You must first take ownership of what led you to where you are now before you can take control of where you end up. This first chapter is a look back in the rearview mirror. Defining your current situation and how you got here is crucial before you can begin your journey to academic success.

Another important consideration on this road trip is whom you are bringing with you. Although it is your journey, you should consider the company you keep along the way. Will you include a whiney co-pilot who always complains about the music you're playing or which direction you choose to go? Would your trip be more enjoyable if you are receiving positive support from people with multiple perspectives? You also need snacks for energy! Consider what you will use to energize yourself when the road seems never-ending or full of speed bumps and potholes. You may need to make multiple pit-stops for gas, get help from strangers for directions, or find new parts to replace broken ones. You do not need to navigate this journey, and all the problem solving that comes with it, alone; you can and should turn to others for help along the way.

Checkpoint

Every good road trip needs a good playlist. Let's start with creating your own soundtrack or theme song for your journey. Write something inspirational. Maybe it's a quote, a song lyric that makes you smile, or a supportive or comforting phrase a loved one or mentor shared with you. It is important to keep it positive, inspiring, and personal.

_____

_____

_____

Now write these inspirational words on the inside cover of this book, as a reminder to keep going as you progress through the book and your semester. This book is yours, but more important, your thoughts are under your control and should be focused on what you are capable of achieving, not how you may have gotten lost along the way.

Maybe you are the spontaneous type. You do not use maps, you just go with the flow, turn where you want to turn, and end up wherever the road takes you. Being spontaneous and flexible is very different than moving along your route without purpose. It may feel overwhelming to look so far into the future. Maybe you are struggling academically because you are unsure about your major or why you need a college degree. Maybe your current situation was triggered by a financial crisis. Whatever your situation may be, this book is made for you.

As you go through this book you will have opportunities to personalize each chapter with your current plan and how you will meet your intended targets. As you're reading, you will pause and complete Checkpoints as an opportunity to confirm your understanding before you continue reading. As you progress through the chapter, pull over, take a break, and consider how the subject you are reading about applies to you. This break is a Scenic Overlook from your perspective. Application of the lessons learned is found in the many activities throughout each chapter. The pages are perforated to allow you to easily tear out the pages as necessary. Finally, in addition to ending each chapter with a conclusion and post-chapter questions, you'll find the Rev Your Engine as the additional challenge you were looking for, in order to delve deeper into a particular subject. So, rev your engines and get started — it's time for the rubber to meet the road.

THE NUMBERS

What is your current academic situation?

On a road trip, it would be helpful to be able to read a map and know your longitude and latitude coordinates. In identifying your current academic situation, the number you need to be aware of is your grade point average (GPA). Your GPA is the measurement that may have created a detour along your academic success journey.

GPA: A magical illusion or simple math?

Have you…
- o   Skipped a few classes?
- o   Not completed your homework whether it was graded or not?
- o   Avoided studying for tests because the material overwhelmed you?
- o   Denied you needed any additional help when it was offered?
- o   Worked more hours than you could balance in your week?
- o   Struggled with personal health issues temporarily or long-term?

There are countless reasons that may have led you to your current **academic standing**. Although a successful college experience is based on a number of factors, there are minimal expectations you are expected to satisfy to continue on to graduation. Graduation and the opportunity to continue at a college or university are measured by a numeric value, your GPA.

At many colleges and universities, GPA is based on a 4.0 scale. This is calculated by dividing the total amount of grade points earned by the total amount of credit hours attempted.

Your grade point average may range from 0.0 to a 4.0. Generally speaking, here are the grade points associated with letter grades, which may vary.

Grade Points

1.0 = Ds
2.0 = Cs
3.0 = Bs
4.0 = As

The saying "Ds get Degrees" cannot apply universally because most schools of higher education require a 2.0 GPA or higher to graduate. You should be aware of minimum GPA requirements at your institution in order for you to graduate. You should also be aware of the required GPA requirement in your specific major.

Understanding how GPA is calculated directly influences your understanding of where you are and what you need to earn (your goal GPA). For you, the goal GPA may directly influence your academic standing if your current GPA put you in poor academic standing.

Important Terms

Poor versus Good Academic Standing is defined by your individual college. There is a minimum GPA you must maintain before a student is placed on probation or is dismissed. Poor academic standing would be below this minimum standard and a good academic standing would be at or above it. This GPA may also be specific to the number of credits you have earned.

Grade Points are a numerical value assigned to a letter grade received in a course at a college or university, which is then multiplied by the number of credits awarded for the course.

Credit Hours are units of measuring educational credit, usually based on the number of classroom hours per week throughout a term (semester).

Total Quality Hours is obtained by multiplying a course's credit hours by numerical value of the grade assigned (grade points).

Cumulative GPA is your calculated average of grades from all earned hours. In many cases transfer credit, credits earned from testing, or any other credits that were not earned for a grade at your current college could count toward your overall earned hours, but not toward your Cumulative GPA.

Semester GPA is the calculated average of grades from all hours earned in a specific semester.

Goal GPA is the cumulative GPA you are working toward. For our purposes, your goal GPA is specific to what your college policy states you need to be in good standing.

Target GPA is the Semester GPA of your currently enrolled courses that is required to earn in order to bring your cumulative GPA to your goal GPA at the end of the semester.

Overall Earned versus Overall GPA Hours is defined by which credits were successfully completed at your college. Credits successfully transferred to your college will count toward your Overall Earned Hours, in addition to all credits from the courses you passed at your current college. Overall GPA Hours include all credit hours completed at your college that specifically count toward your GPA, regardless if you passed or not.

Checkpoint

Why is GPA important to colleges and how is it calculated?

_____

_____

_____

_____

You must identify your goal GPA based on the minimum GPA required for you to return to good standing. You also need to consider other academic standards, major requirements, athletic demands, and financial aid conditions.

When you review final grades at the end of the semester, keep in mind you earned that grade. Your grade calculation begins on Day One of the class, when the syllabus is given to you. The syllabus you receive for every class is a contract that outlines all the stipulations of your future earned grade, including what specifically counts for a grade, how each of those graded items is weighted, and what scale your letter grade is based on per course. If you find yourself not knowing your grade in a class, don't blame the **professors** for not updating you daily with this information. It is your responsibility to keep track of your grades. Find the page in your syllabus with information about grades and how grades are weighted and note each grade as you receive it to keep track.

At the end of the semester, your grade is in the form of a percentage. The grading scale found in your syllabus is used to translate your percentage into a letter grade. For example, an 82% final grade may be equivalent to a B or C+, depending on the individual professor's grading scale. You have seen letter grades in school since you have been learning the alphabet and they are still A, B, C, D, or F with pluses and minuses (this may vary by institution).

Checkpoint

You earned a C in a 3-credit-hour course, now complete the following equation.

C = _____ grade points

_____ credit hours x _____ grade points = _____ quality hours

YOUR GPA AND FINANCIAL AID

By Kate Tiller

It is important to know and understand that your **academic standing** may affect your financial aid. If you do not pay for school in its entirety, you may have loans, grants, or scholarships. Everyone's financial aid is a bit different, and there should be experts in your school's financial aid office who can help you navigate your current standing and how it affects your financial aid.

There is a law that states that all students receiving federal or state (and some institutional) financial aid are required to meet **Satisfactory Academic Progress** (SAP). SAP is a set of standards set by your school that require you earn enough hours and high enough grades to stay on your school's standard of a reasonable pace toward earning your degree.

This program falls under the U.S. Department of Education's Office of Federal Student Aid, and if you are not in good academic standing at your school, you may be in danger of not meeting SAP. The program's website explains that your school's policy should tell you:

- what grade-point average (or equivalent standard) you need to maintain;
- how quickly you need to be moving toward graduation (for instance, how many credits you should have successfully completed by the end of each year);
- how an incomplete class, withdrawal, repeated class, change of major, or transfer of credits from another school affects your **satisfactory academic progress**;
- how often your school will evaluate your progress;
- what will happen if you fail to make **satisfactory academic progress** when your school evaluates you;
- whether you are allowed to appeal your school's decision that you haven't made **satisfactory academic progress** (reasons for appeal usually include the death of a member of your family, your illness or injury, or other special circumstances); and
- how you can regain eligibility for federal student aid.[1]

Beyond SAP, there are a few other important financial aid considerations:
- The standards set forth in your school's SAP policy may be lower than requirements for certain scholarships that you've been awarded. Be aware of all the requirements for maintaining and renewing all your aid.
- Always read emails or other correspondence from your financial aid office and act on them promptly. Processes handled in this department are often time sensitive.
- Read any terms and conditions that are part of accepting your financial aid. It is important to know what you are agreeing to by accepting your aid.
- Fill out the FAFSA (Free Application for Federal Student Aid) each year.

Checkpoint

Answer the following questions using necessary resources. You need to have access to viewing your updated grades and GPA. This may be obtained from an online degree audit system, an unofficial academic transcript, or by working with your academic advisor.

Current Cumulative GPA:	
Overall Earned Hours:	
Overall GPA Hours:	
Total Quality Hours:	
Transfer Hours Earned:	
Major GPA (if declared):	
GPA required for Financial Aid or other requirements:	
Best Semester GPA in College:	
This semester's goal GPA:	

GPA calculation is a formula and there are numerous online calculators for you to use, but it is important to understand how GPA is calculated. It is not a magic equation your professors or administrators keep secret from you to engage students in a guessing game. If you consider your road trip, you always know a gas station exists ahead of you somewhere and you always see signs for one when you're not looking for them. When you see the flashing "E" and panic because you haven't seen a pit-stop in miles, you want to know which upcoming exit has a gas station, how many miles ahead the exit is, and approximately how many miles you can travel on "E" without coming to a stop. To plan ahead for how you are going to arrive at your Goal GPA, you need to know what you must earn this semester (Target GPA) to get back on the right track.

Name _____ Date _____

ACTIVITY: GPA CALCULATION _ _ _ _ _ _ _ _ _ _ _ _ _ _ _

Use your current semester courses to complete the chart below and calculate your current semester's future GPA. You may need to refer to the previous checkpoint to complete the chart.

Subject	Goal Letter Grade	Quality Points x	Credit Hours =	Total Quality Points for course
(e.g.) Biology 101	C	2.0	4	8.0

Quality Points per Grade (Check with your institution's policy)			
A = 4.0	B = 3.0	C = 2.0	D = 1.0
A- = 3.7	B- = 2.7	C- = 1.7	D- = 0.7
B+ = 3.3	C+ = 2.3	D+ = 1.3	F = 0.0

Semester TOTAL   (A) _____   (B) _____
                        Credit Hours   Quality Points

Semester GPA = _____
                       (B ÷ A)

Projected Cumulative GPA at End of Semester:

Total Quality Points   ÷   *Total Quality Hours*   =   *GPA*

Total Quality Points this semester	_____ (B)		Total Credit Hours this semester	_____ (A)	
	+			+	
Quality Points to date	_____ =		Quality Hours attempted to date*	_____ =	
Total	_____	÷	Total	_____ =	

* Quality Hours are the total number of credit hours attempted at your college, including failed courses, but excluding withdrawals.

CHAPTER 1: Checking the Engine: A Reality Check -

Did calculating your GPA by hand change your perspective? You will likely use online GPA calculators from now on, but at least the calculation is no longer a mystery. Think of something that you may take for granted, such as electricity. Growing up, you may have left lights on in every room and not thought twice about it, but after you pay the first bill and understand the cost of leaving those lights on, you begin to think twice about your use. When you set a specific target GPA for a semester or a goal cumulative GPA, it will mean more to you if you know how it was calculated and what it means for the specific grades you need to earn in a semester. Does knowing how something works help you appreciate it more?

MAPPING YOUR STORY

What led you to this current academic situation? Everyone has a story. When you first meet someone, what types of questions do you ask them? You may ask where they are from or where they went to school; you're looking to get to know them. When you're on a road trip, strangers are often curious to know what brought you to your current location and other stops made along the way. Have you thought about how this related to your academic journey?

You know when you lose your keys or wallet or something of value, usually you ask yourself — when did I last have that item? Can I remember what I was doing, where I was, or what I did next? In order to answer these questions, you retrace your steps, you may have to work backwards and remember back to a few hours ago or a few days ago. You may find it easy to remember when you last had your keys and replay in your mind the details of what happened next. In panic, you may put blame on someone else, even though you are the one who lost something of value. Whichever way you process information, looking back, remembering, and taking responsibility for what you did with those keys is an important step to finding them again.

You are currently in a position of academic deficiency, which can be measured by a number of factors, such as your GPA you just calculated. However, you did not begin your college career this way. You may have seen your path to poor academic standing coming from a distance. You knew the decisions you were making would lead you down this path and the grades you were earning would eventually catch up to you. Or maybe you didn't see it coming at all. You were a successful student in previous semesters, at a previous college, or in high school. This situation of poor academic standing is not something you have even come to grasp yet because it is so unlike you. You might even be in denial about your academic standing, saying to yourself that your GPA isn't the best, but it certainly isn't as bad as your roommate's. Wherever you're standing right now, it is important to realize that your keys are lost and you need to begin the process of retracing your steps to make sure you find them and prevent any chance of losing them again.

Calculating your GPA put your current academic standing into a perspective that is measurable. However, more than your grades and following a formula of calculations influences college and academic success. Not all students end up in academic deficiency because they are poor students. Life happens. You may have been so caught up in the immediacy of getting into college that you did not realize all the changes taking place before you. Maybe you were challenged by financial restraints. You might have been working two jobs and unable to find a balance between paying bills and paying attention to your coursework. You may be dependent on financial aid to assist you in your education, but your lump sum of money did not hit your bank account in time to purchase books until you were already too far behind in the class to catch up. Your health may have taken a drastic nosedive, which required time away from school. It could even have been the health of a close family member or friend. Maybe this added stress prevented you from putting school as a first priority. Speaking of family, your loved ones may have put unreachable expectations on you to succeed in college and life and you only felt like you were disappointing them. Your family may not have supported your decision to move away and leave them in order to attend college. While away at college, maybe you have been challenged by balancing relationships with a significant other near or far. You may have been working toward a major with required courses that did not align with your strengths or your interests. There are an endless number of reasons that students may find themselves in a situation of academic deficiency.

Everyone has a story; no one goes through life with the same experiences. There is no correct and perfect path to a college degree. Whatever your story, own it. Don't let your story be your excuse. Your story, your experience, the decisions you made, all brought you to where you currently stand and you'll need to look back at them to make changes going forward.

As you travel and go about living your life, you are absorbed in the daily activities of the trip. While driving, you are focused on the destination. You get caught up in the immediacy of the trip and it is not until you have had a chance to stop that you realize you are not even sure what roads you took to get here. You did not consciously think of how fast you were going, what lane you were in, the turns you made, and the exits you missed. Your passengers were concerned about the music choice or they may have attempted to help you find your way, but you ignored their help. After all, you've been driving for years! Does this sound familiar?

As you look back on your journey to your current situation, you may or may not be able to pinpoint the events that led you to this point of academic deficiency. It is time to look at a map, consider where you began, and identify how you got to where you are now, so you can create a new path forward.

CRITICAL SELF-REFLECTION

By Melissa Hortman

Throughout this book you will be asked to reflect on content, experiences, and other aspects of your life. Life happens but taking the time to reflect on it and contextualize experiences helps the learning potential of the situation. Through self-reflection there are thoughts and feelings that emerge which can help you to generalize the experience to then tackle new situations more effectively. Below you can see the steps you need to take when thinking through a reflective writing prompt.

What happened? → **Why/how did it happen?** → **What's your new interpretation of the experience?** → **How will you use it to inform your future?**

As you take time to go through each of the steps in the process of a reflection, you need to take yourself out of the box of the standard, academic essay you may have written for other courses. Self-reflection is a different way to think and write than you may be used to, therefore here are some points of what self-reflection is and is not.

Self-reflection is:	Self-reflection is not:
a way of making meaning out of what you study.	just conveying information.
a way to achieve clarity.	purely a description.
an opportunity to gain self-knowledge.	a straightforward decision or judgment.
a way of thinking to explore your learning.	a summary of course content.
your response to experiences or new information.	a standard academic essay.

To critically self-reflect we need to think about it within the context of the words.

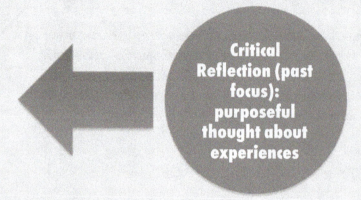

Critical Reflection (past focus): purposeful thought about experiences

Critical reflection is the connection between currently thinking about the past so as to impact future decision-making. There are many different ways you can write reflectively. Reflective writing can be personal, hypothetical, critical, and creative in style. Following are some ideas on what you can write about in your reflective writing.

- Discuss experiences you had in the past and how they relate to the course or topic; tell a story to bring the reader into your personal life.
- Discuss relationships and connections between what you are learning through the prompt and:
  - your previous knowledge and experience;
  - your previous assumptions and biases;
  - knowledge from other courses or disciplines.
- Discuss areas you found confusing, inspiring, challenging, or interesting and why you felt that way.
- Discuss how you solved a problem, reached a conclusion, found an answer, or reached a point of understanding after an experience or as you are drawing connections in your writing.
- Discuss alternative interpretations or perspectives on reading or discussions in your course.

Try to take your writing to the next level when writing reflectively by beginning to see the same actions or events in different contexts with different explanations. Reflective writing is a way of helping you become an active, aware, and critical learner as you reflect on experiences and try to get back on track in your journey.

YOUR TURN TO MAP

The ability to extract yourself and reflect on your current situation begins now. This chapter is your pit-stop to look at your own map and the route you have taken until this point in your academic standing.

Similar to what you do when you lose your keys; begin where you feel most comfortable. This may be a chronological timeline of events or a myriad of visuals to represent your story. You may begin where you are standing right now and retrace your steps as you discover singular events that lead you back to where your motivation to succeed in college began. You may begin your map years ago, possibly even middle or high school or your academic experiences prior to college. You'll map your route including events and people, in addition to the decisions you made that led you to your current position. Include experiences you consider to have directly or inadvertently led you to where you are now. This includes the small decisions you made every day or epic milestones that define you. Include the good, the bad, and the ugly — this is your map, so make it meaningful to you.

Checkpoint

Here are some highlights you may choose to include in your map. Check all that you will include in your map and add any others not listed.

- ❏ When you first knew you were going to attend college
- ❏ Difference between high school and college expectations
- ❏ Your transition to college
- ❏ Specific classes you enrolled in (i.e., _____)
- ❏ Colleges you transferred to/from
- ❏ Teachers, professors, with positive and negative impacts on your success
- ❏ Friends and family with positive and negative impacts on your success
- ❏ Health issues
- ❏ How you spent time if you left college for a period of time
- ❏ Family events
- ❏ Relationships
- ❏ Times when you sought help
- ❏ Midterm and final grades
- ❏ _____
- ❏ _____
- ❏ _____

Name _____ Date _____

ACTIVITY: MAPPING YOUR STORY_ _ _ _ _ _ _ _ _ _ _ _ _

On this page, illustrate the map you have already traveled. The focus should be your **academic standing**, while considering inside and outside the classroom experiences that led you to your current position. There are many highlights to include, but this is your story — it should make sense to you. This is a visual representation, YOUR visual representation of your journey.

Scenic Overlook

Take a look at your visual representation. Take in the entire work as a piece of art, paying close attention to details and the decisions you made in its construction. As one would do when looking at art, interpret meaning from your visualization. Think about the decisions you made on what event to start with, how to visually represent your story, to use the whole page or just part of it. Does interpreting your visualization give it even greater meaning?

WRITE YOUR STORY

Storytelling is a timeless human tradition and a crucial skill in your journey toward success. It is the art of attaching a human face and an emotion to a personal experience. Stories have the power to make connections you never saw before because you did not take the time to extract yourself from the situation. Stories can help formulate new ideas and help persuade you to see yourself in a new perspective. Stories also have the power to motivate.

Checkpoint

What is a motivating story you remember?

_____

_____

_____

What made it motivating to you?

_____

_____

Your story is always a work in progress. It is a messy, complicated, and ongoing journey. You may not know how your story will end and you may be terrified of the blank pages ahead, but take ownership of your story because it is yours to write.

This is your time to practice written communication and storytelling. The purpose is to be honest with yourself about the previous experiences that directly or inadvertently led you to where you are now. You may have included these in your visual map because they were a milestone or a huge obstacle you were challenged by. Also include experiences you may have left out of your visual map, possibly an experience you don't believe to be monumental but provides a better context for your life and your academic journey.

Name _____ Date _____

ACTIVITY: WRITING YOUR STORY _____

Provide a written story of your visual map. This is a context of who you are and where you have been. The additional expectation to the written storytelling, not found in the visual, is thoughtful reflection. You are not merely listing all the events and happenings found in your map, you must analyze how you see them impacting each other and how they led you to your current position.

_____

_____

_____

_____

_____

_____

_____

_____

_____

_____

_____

_____

_____

_____

_____

_____

_____

_____

SHARING YOUR STORY _____

Where are you going and how will get you there?

You've written your story and now you need to share it. When you are in a town you've never been before, you talk to the locals. They find out about your road trip and based on what they know about you and what you are hoping to accomplish, they will make helpful recommendations for the best places to eat, a unique attraction you must see, and tips for finding the most scenic route to your next stop! You too can gain insight from the people around you if they know where you are headed. In your story, you are the compelling character; therefore you should act the part. You want to engage with your audience to get the best response, which may mean communicating with the student sitting next to you in class, your current professors, your academic advisor, and additional campus resources. They should know your name. Don't be another face in the classroom. Get your story out there.

WHAT EXACTLY IS A PROFESSOR?
By Kate Tiller

Let's talk about college professors. Who are these people? College **professors** have studied their disciplines and continue to study and learn about them through their research every day. After many years of study, they are considered to be experts in their fields. Many of them are extremely passionate about their subject matter and want to share it with their students.

Many professors have earned their master's and doctorate degrees. This means that after they completed their undergraduate education, they went on to graduate school in a specific area of study. A master's degree usually requires around two additional years of school and some sort of thesis or capstone research project in the field. Earning a doctorate involves study past the master's level and the writing of a dissertation, a scholarly examination of some previously unaddressed facet in the respective field of study. A doctorate is usually the highest degree a person can earn in his field. So, you are in the class of a person who is highly knowledgeable and who has devoted a lot of his or her life to the subject, and you have an opportunity to learn a lot from this individual.

What do professors do when they are not teaching your class? Many professors teach a full class load, hold office hours (which we will talk about later), serve on campus committees, mentor or advise students, and research and write. Professors are usually part of a tenure system where Professors or Associate Professors are the senior-most positions. Some professors are assistant professors working to become tenured. You might have a professor called an adjunct professor who teaches part-time and does not have the same institutional responsibilities as other professors. Regardless of where your professor stands professionally, it is important to remember that professors are people, too! They have families, friends, commitments, and responsibilities outside of their work just like you.

Professors usually list their office hours on their course syllabus. This is the time that they are available for their students to come talk with them, and most professors actually want to see their students then! If you have a question about the class or an upcoming assignment, going to office hours is a great way to get some extra help. Your professors can help you evaluate your study style, note-taking strategies, and suggest ways to maximize your time in their specific classes or disciplines. You can even go to office hours just to introduce yourself and get to know your professors in a slightly different way.

Finally, on a practical note, knowing what to call your professors can be a little tricky. Some professors will tell you exactly what they want to be called; some might even ask you to call them by their first name. If you have professors who do not explicitly provide a preference, you can look at their syllabi or profiles online, if one is available, to see if they have a PhD at the end of their names. If they do, then you know that it is appropriate to call them "*Dr. [Last Name]*." If you still are not sure, calling your professors "*Professor [Last Name]*" is always appropriate.

MEET YOUR PROFESSORS

Striking up conversation with someone you have only met once or twice can be challenging. This may be especially intimidating when this someone is your professor, an expert in their field and the person who grades your exams. Many of them traveled a similar journey just like the one you are on now. Remember, your professors are the locals and can make helpful recommendations based on your questions, but only if you ask! You'll find that your professors want you to be successful and can be helpful resources in reaching your goals.

Before you attend an appointment or visit scheduled office hours, have a game plan. You should be respectful and know what to call them, identify who you are and what class you are in. Professors may not be able to recall your face without any hints from you. Have a list of questions that you want to ask. You can prepare these questions by considering what you want to know about your professor, if their class is related to a career or major of interest, or how they got into teaching. Discuss your interest in doing well in the course, the grade you plan to earn, and ask about specific advice. This meeting breaks the ice before you return later in the semester to discuss your progress toward your goal grade. This meeting will also demonstrate to your professor that you care about the course and your grade. An extra benefit is now your professor knows who you are!

Checkpoint

Name 4 reasons to meet your professors during office hours or scheduled appointment.

_____

_____

_____

_____

EMAIL ETIQUETTE IS ESSENTIAL
By Kate Tiller

Emailing is one of the primary forms of communication used on college campuses. You probably get a lot of email from your campus on a daily basis, alerting you to events that are going on or to important information you need to know. Your official school email account is often the way that professors or other professional staff on campus will communicate with you. The number one rule of email etiquette is that you should check your official email regularly and be responsible for the information you are provided in your emails.

There are some other important things to think about when emailing faculty or staff on your campus. Here are some general rules:

1. **Email**, especially the first time you email someone, is a formal correspondence. Do not fall into the trap of treating email like a text message with your friends! You should use correct grammar and punctuation. Run a spell check and re-read your email before you send it. Also, if you are sending an email when you are feeling upset or angry about the subject matter, it is a good idea to write the email, then save it in your "draft" messages and wait a little while before you send it. Once you have hit *Send*, you cannot take your words back.

2. Whatever you do, do not leave the subject blank. Some professors might outline in their syllabi what they expect to see in your subject line. If not, it is helpful to reference your name and, if possible, the nature of your request. If you are emailing a professor, including the name of the class or the section number is also a good idea.
    EX: Subject: Janie Jackson-ENGL110.004-Meeting Request
    EX: Subject: Financial Aid Question – Joe Smith

3. Address the person you're emailing properly. Using a salutation like *Dear* is very formal and appropriate, but if you have a less formal relationship, you could start with *Hello* or *Hi.*
    If you are emailing a professor, address him or her using the proper title like *Dr.* or *Professor.* You may be emailing an academic dean; if you are, you could refer to that person as *Dean.* If you are emailing a staff member on campus who might not have a title like those, you can use *Mr.* or *Ms.* Using *Ms.* is an appropriate way to address a woman without assuming anything about her marital status. If you cannot figure out exactly whom you are emailing, you can start with something like "*Good Morning.*"
    EX: Dear Dr. Williams,
    EX: Hi Professor Taylor,
    EX: Hello Ms. Johnson,

4. Introduce who you are, especially if this is your first email to a recipient with whom you do not have a close relationship. This can be short and sweet like *I am John Smith from your 8 a.m. English class.* You want to provide a point of reference. After emailing back and forth with someone consistently, this becomes less important. Or, if you know the person really well, you would not need to be this formal.

5. Most of the time if you are emailing someone on campus, you are emailing for a specific reason or because you have a specific request. Make sure that your request or reason is clear. Also remember that it is important to be polite and sincere in your email. Though you cannot see the recipient when you are emailing, you are emailing another person who is going to feel something based on what you say and how you say it. Again, USE CORRECT GRAMMAR!

6. End your request with a closing and your name. It is often nice, but not necessary to include your campus identification number (so they can look up you and information related to your request) and other contact information.
   EX: Sincerely, (or Thank you,)
   Jack Smith
   10301010
   jjsmith1@yourcollege.edu

Scenic Overlook

When you first communicate with a faculty member via email, this is their first impression of you. First impressions greatly influence how one is treated and viewed. The tone you set in the email, whether on purpose or without intention should represent how you wish to be remembered. If you do not include your name, you may not be remembered at all. If you use too many !!!!!! it may be read like you are yelling. How would you interpret a message from someone who didn't spell your name correctly? Emails and other forms of communication are challenging to convey emotion without the non-verbal cues, but there are ways to set a good first impression. How can you convey a good first impression through email communication?

CONCLUSION

You are beginning a road trip. Before you take off in a direction of your choosing, you must consider where you want to go and where you have already been. You must be able to define your academic standing and target the factors that led you to this position. Your GPA is a numeric measurement colleges and universities use to define your ability to progress and graduate. Awareness of your GPA requirements and the target GPA you need will specifically address how to get back into good standing. Taking time to reflect on your previous experiences and taking responsibility for your actions is the first time in making changes necessary to achieve your goals. There are many resources around your college campus created to support your goal of academic success. Visit your professors, ask questions, schedule appointments with academic advisors. Take time to consider the role your professors play on campus and professionally communicate with them.

"Those who cannot remember the past are condemned to repeat it."
~ George Santayana

Rev Your Engine

You have prepared your story and looked ahead to where you want to end up. This semester, it is important to share your story and reach out to resources on campus, such as your professors. You now have reviewed appropriate ways to communicate with your professors and it is time to go meet them. To take the next step in communicating with your professors, you will interview one of your professors in one of your most challenging courses this semester. Then, you can continue this assignment with all your other professors.

Professor Interview Assignment:
   a. Identify your professor and make a plan of when you will meet with them.
   b. Create a list of questions for the interview preparation.
   c. Write a 2- to 4-page essay summarizing and reflecting on the content of the interview. Share what you learned from your professor and reflect on how you plan to move forward.

CITATIONS

Baxter Magolda, M. B. (2009). *Authoring your life: Developing an internal voice to navigate life's challenges.* Sterling, VA: Stylus Publishing Company.

Brookfield, S. (1987). *Developing critical thinkers: Challenging adults to explore alternative ways of thinking and acting.* San Francisco, CA: Jossey-Bass.

Mezirow, J. (1990). *Fostering critical reflection in adulthood: A guide to transformative and emancipatory learning.* San Francisco, CA: Jossey-Bass.

Schön, D.A. (1987). *Educating the reflective practitioner.* San Francisco, CA: Jossey-Bass.

"Staying Eligible," Retrieved from https://studentaid.ed.gov/eligibility/staying-eligible

Post Test/Quiz

1. Define credit hour.

2. Explain the purpose of a target GPA.

3. What is critical reflection?

4. True or False: Self-Reflection writing examples include a summary of material and exclude your response to information.

5. True of False: Self-Reflection is a way to make your own meaning from events and information and a way to gain self-knowledge.

6. Where can you find your professor's office hours?

7. Name at least 3 items you should always include in an email to your professor.

CHAPTER 2

CHECKING YOUR MIRRORS: EXAMINING YOUR PAST AND CREATING YOUR FUTURE

By Cristy Landis and Lindy Coleman

1. LEARNING OUTCOMES: QUESTIONS TO NAVIGATE
   a. Can you define what will motivate you to achieve academic good standing and graduate from college?
   b. What factors have gotten you off track in the past?
   c. What does your roadmap to success look like?
   d. Are you utilizing accountability partners both in and outside class to help you achieve your goals?
   e. Can you define values and determine what your own values are, using Maslow's Hierarchy of Needs?
   f. How would you link your core values to your achievement of a college degree?
   g. What is your understanding of the concept of self-actualization as it pertains to your own personal growth and development as a college student?

2. KEY CONCEPTS
   a. Accountability
   b. Motivation
   c. Goal setting and purposeful action
   d. Maslow's Hierarchy of Needs
   e. Self-Actualization
   f. Core values
   g. Locus of Control
   h. Fixed mindset versus growth mindset
   i. Neuroplasticity of the brain
   j. Flow

INTRODUCTION _

You've got the route planned out, your bags packed, and you're ready to roll out of town. But wait — did you check everything? Will you have enough gas for the whole trip or will you need to stop periodically and re-fuel? Have you checked your mirrors so you can have a clear vision of what may be creeping up on you from behind and what lies ahead? Thinking ahead, troubleshooting, and planning will make the trip safer and help you reach your desired destination.

The same is true with your college journey. Do you have enough gas — that is, motivation — to carry you through? How will you re-fuel yourself? Have you taken the time to reflect on previous challenges, so they won't sabotage you again? Can you see your vision for your future self and have you cleared a path to achieve it? Doing these things involves a great deal of honest introspection and self-reflection. Sometimes this is painful — we don't like to think about those things that steered us off the path — and sometimes it is scary — what will my future life look like? But it is worth it! Taking the time now to think about and plan your trip toward academic recovery will ensure that this time you reach your goal.

DESTINATION: GRADUATION! MOTIVATION? _ _ _ _ _ _ _

You know that your destination goal is college graduation. But what is going to keep you on the path this time? First, you need to determine your **motivation**.

Establishing and sustaining motivation for academic success is a real challenge for some college students. While some students seem to know what they want from college and pursue it from their first semester to their last, others start strong, then lose interest and focus, and, subsequently, lose academic ground. While you may choose a variety of paths and have different goals during your college career, you need to determine what is important to you and what will keep you going until you achieve it.

There are two types of motivation: **intrinsic**, which means doing things because they give you personal satisfaction and enjoyment; and **extrinsic**, which refers to doing or not doing things because of potential repercussions, such as a reward for completing a task or a punishment for failing to do a job. Why should this matter to you? Because what motivates you has much to do with how you persist to reach your goal. You may have started strong, with the best intentions in the world but failed to follow through to your destination. In order to turn things around, you need to understand why you ran off the road the first time, and how you are going to stay on the road this time!

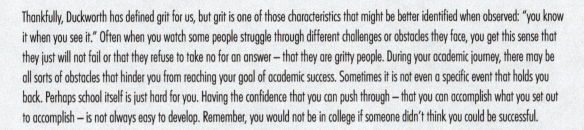

KEEP ON KEEPING ON: GRIT AND PERSEVERANCE
By Kate Tiller

Angela Duckworth, an Associate Professor of Psychology at the University of Pennsylvania, devotes her research to the concept of grit. In *Grit: Perseverance and Passion for Long-Term Goals*, Duckworth and fellow researchers define grit:

> We define grit as perseverance and passion for long-term goals. Grit entails working strenuously toward challenges, maintaining effort and interest over years despite failure, adversity, and plateaus in progress. The gritty individual approaches achievement as a marathon; his or her advantage is stamina.

Thankfully, Duckworth has defined grit for us, but grit is one of those characteristics that might be better identified when observed: "you know it when you see it." Often when you watch some people struggle through different challenges or obstacles they face, you get this sense that they just will not fail or that they refuse to take no for an answer — that they are gritty people. During your academic journey, there may be all sorts of obstacles that hinder you from reaching your goal of academic success. Sometimes it is not even a specific event that holds you back. Perhaps school itself is just hard for you. Having the confidence that you can push through — that you can accomplish what you set out to accomplish — is not always easy to develop. Remember, you would not be in college if someone didn't think you could be successful.

The game of baseball provides an often-used example of the confidence needed to be gritty. We have all heard that baseball is a game of failure and that a player can be considered great for hitting the ball 3 out of 10 times at the plate. If these players are only going to get a hit 3 times out of 10, why do they keep going up to bat? What makes them think they are going to hit the ball every time they step up to the plate? Because of the time they spend practicing, honing their technique, and even learning from the last time they struck out, good hitters are able to develop a belief that they will hit the next pitch. In the same way, the pitcher on the mound, because of similar preparation, believes that his next pitch will be a strike. Confidence in your preparation is part of developing the grit you need to achieve your goals. Everything you are learning in this text, when put to practice, will help you when the next curve ball is thrown your way. That confidence will not always be unwavering; continuing the example, you will strike out. Maybe you will fail a test you really thought you aced and you might feel like you will never recover. When your confidence seems to be waning, returning to techniques and strategies you have developed will help you regain your footing and begin to feel more confident about your ability to face your challenge.

Having the confidence in yourself that you can beat the obstacle at hand, no matter what, is one part of grit. Persistence — tenacity, resolve, perseverance — is another part of grit. Grit is taking on all the challenges and distractions you might run into on your road trip — having a flat tire, running out of gas, getting lost — and still pushing through until you reach your final destination. It can be exhausting to never give up, but people who never give up on what they want are more likely to achieve their goals than people who let obstacles or distractions get in their way of success.

ACTIVITY

Goal Setting Grid: For each of the listed categories, answer all the questions in the spaces provided pertaining to your goals/aspirations and how you plan to achieve them.

	Academics	Interpersonal Relationships	Health & Wellness	Money & Finances	Other _____
What do you want?					
Why do you want it?					
How can you get it?					

	Academics	Interpersonal Relationships	Health & Wellness	Money & Finances	Other _____
What obstacles might get in your way?					
What will you do to stay on your path when the going gets tough?					
What will it take for you to achieve the success you want?					
When will you achieve this goal?					

SETTING A GOAL

By Kate Tiller

When you set out on a road trip, you probably have a specific destination or purpose in mind. These goals might range from seeing certain sights to meeting up with old friends to reaching a certain place at a specific time. This purpose or destination is a goal, a specific outcome that you would like to reach. Knowing how to set a goal is an important skill that will help you as you determine how to reach your academic potential.

There are many goal-setting techniques out there that can help you when you are trying to figure out how to set a goal. If you conduct an Internet search for *"How to set a goal,"* you will find many suggestions. An example of one such guide, created by Skip Downing in his academic success book, *On Course* is called DAPPS:

Dated - Motivating goals have specific deadlines.

Achievable - Motivating goals are challenging but realistic.

Personal - Motivating goals are *your* goals, not someone else's.

Positive - Motivating goals focus your energy on what you *do* want rather than on what you *don't* want.

Specific - Motivating goals state outcomes in specific measurable terms.

Before you set a goal, you should think about what you want and consider if it is reasonable and achievable. If it is not, that does not mean you should abandon that desire! It simply means you should break that goal down into smaller, more achievable parts. Think about when you want to reach your goal. Again, if the outcome you are looking for is in the distant future, you may want to set benchmarks or smaller goals that you can look forward to reaching sooner. Reaching little milestones along the way will help you remain more engaged in the journey to reach your ultimate goal. Most people will say that you should be able to measure your goal. Specifically, what do you want? How will you know when you have gotten what you wanted?

Here's an example of all those tips in action. You are in an academic recovery course, so you know you want to improve academically. Yet that is a pretty general desire. How can you change that into something more specific? Maybe in the first chapter, Reality Check, you determined that you need a specific GPA to return to good academic standing at your school. So, a measurable and specific goal for the semester might be: will earn a 2.0 GPA by the end of the semester. You have a time frame and a specific number that you are shooting for. However, that goal might be a little too broad and far away. There are shorter term goals that you could set to reach that semester-long goal, like: "I will turn in every homework assignment this week" or "I will not miss any classes this month" or "By midterm, I will have a B average in a specific class or two."

Writing your goals down and posting them where you can see them, as well as verbalizing your intentions to a friend who will help hold you accountable, may help you commit to and successfully achieve your goals.

It might help to know that you're not the only person who has ever struggled with motivation. Academic motivation has been widely researched for decades and the reasons for motivation are linked closely with a number of different theories, including **self-determination theory**, which explores what makes people do what they do or don't do. Psychologists Edward Deci and Richard Ryan (2002) asserted that in order to maintain motivation, individuals need to feel: a) competent in their skills; b) connected to others who will support them; and c) autonomous, or in charge of their own behaviors and goals. Does that sound like you? Do you feel that you possess the knowledge and skills you need to graduate from college? Do you have a community of support, consisting of family, friends, professors, co-workers, or others? Do you feel that you are in control of your own destiny or do things just "happen" to you? If you answered "no" to one or more of these questions, this could explain, at least in part, why staying motivated may be a struggle for you. Part of our work together will be to help you turn each "no" into a "yes"!

WHO IS IN THE DRIVER'S SEAT? _ _ _ _ _ _ _ _ _ _ _ _ _ _ _ _

All of us, as we move through our daily activities, keep a running conversation going with ourselves. Sometimes this may be as mundane as "I need to remember to put another quarter in the meter in 45 minutes" or as important as "My Econ test is this week. I need to do more practice problems!"

Your thoughts impact the decisions you make. What you say to yourself affects the actions you take. The actions you take then create the circumstances of your life. Your actions are largely determined by how you view the world. Some people believe that they are the "masters of their own destiny" while others believe that they are the "victim of circumstance." In the field of psychology, this is called **locus of control**.

Locus really just means location. Where do you locate power in your life? Is it located within you (internally) or located in the outside world (externally)? If you have an internal locus of control then you believe you can make decisions that create an outcome. You are not a victim of fate or someone who relies on luck, instead you act on the belief that what happens to you is a result of decisions you have made. This means that you realize that life presents you with obstacles and that some life events are beyond your control but overall you know that, even when an unexpected event happens, you are in control of how you react to those circumstances.

Take a moment to think about the following questions: Do you believe that what happens to you in your life is a result of fate or because of decisions you make? Do you believe that professors make grading decisions objectively or that your grade is determined by whether or not the professor "likes" you? Is there such a thing as an "unfair test" or does preparing well, attending class, and reviewing material create a positive outcome? Do you feel confident that when you make plans, then take action, you can make things work out or do you feel it is useless to plan because most things turn out to be a matter of luck? Ultimately, do you feel that you have the ability to take control of the direction your life is going?

Research shows that individuals with a strong internal locus of control tend to be happier. They are less anxious and credit their success to their own diligent effort. They are happier both professionally (at work) and interpersonally (in relationships with others). Interestingly enough, people who take responsibility for their actions and the outcomes from those actions also make stronger moral and ethical decisions. Contrast this with the research done on individuals with a strong external locus of control. They are less satisfied with their lives as they move through life feeling out of control and as if the world is "out to get them." They tend to blame others rather than accepting the part they play in their own lives. Rather than taking responsibility for their own decisions, they might abdicate their own power and ascribe it to others saying, "It's not my fault because [fill in the blank]". Their lives are filled with excuses. They tend to blame others, which, of course, has a negative effect on relationships. As you can see, where you locate the power in your life has a tremendous impact on you.

So how do you start building a stronger internal locus of control? First of all, you have to realize that life is about choices (and even seemingly making "no choice" is actually choosing to do or not do something). Each time you are presented with a choice (which actually happens multiple times a day), make sure that you pause a moment to evaluate the pros and cons of each possibility. Ask yourself: "If I choose this over that, what is the likely outcome?" and "What are the long term effects of this choice in addition to the short term gratifications?" Studies show that how people have reacted to circumstances in the past is typically a very strong indicator of how they will react to similar situations in the future. You need to assess if your reactions are **mindful** (do you take time to reflect before making a decision) or have your reactions become more automatic, meaning you have skipped the "thinking" step.

Another way to start building a strong internal locus of control is to pay attention to your own internal monologue (the running conversation you have with yourself during your waking hours). Are you kind to yourself in your "self-talk" or are you overly critical? Do you dwell on thoughts of "I have no choice here" or "this is beyond my control," or do you focus instead on thoughts such as "This happened, so now I get to decide how to react" and "I am capable so I know that I can handle this; I just have to think through the possibilities." It isn't easy to change thought patterns that are ingrained through time but it is definitely possible.

Applying this line of positive thinking to an academic arena leads to a discussion of mindset. Psychologist Carol Dweck has spent her career studying how humans view learning. Consider this: Do you believe that you do well academically because of innate abilities or because of the effort you put forth in your academic tasks? Are you just naturally smart or do you understand that learning is a process and that one can continually improve in a subject area through practice and repetition? Do you believe that your intelligence is fixed and static or do you know that intelligence can be cultivated and then flourish? Individuals with a **fixed mindset** believe that we are born with natural, intrinsic abilities that rarely can be changed. If you think this way, you might hear yourself say, "I'm not a good writer." On the other hand, those with a **growth mindset** believe that the brain is malleable; that one certainly has natural strengths but others can be cultivated. This would manifest with internal self-talk that would sound like: "My writing needs to be developed, so I need to work on improving in that area…I need to go to my campus writing lab or meet with my professor." With a growth mindset, you know that neuroscientists have proven that the brain is malleable; it has **neuroplasticity**, meaning that your brain grows and develops throughout your life based on your experiences. You increase your understanding of a subject by immersing yourself in learning about that subject — in short — by practicing that information.

KNOW YOURSELF
By Kate Tiller

You know that feeling you get when you are doing something you know you are good at? You feel accomplished, at ease, and you have everything under control. Sometimes in sports, people refer to being "in the zone" when they are performing at their best — hitting shot after shot or making a great play.

Donald Clifton, considered to be the "father of strengths-based psychology and the grandfather of positive psychology," researched the importance of people knowing their strengths and engaging in activities where they can use those strengths. In response to Clifton's research, Timothy Hodges and James Hartner say: "Strengths development begins with individuals recognizing and psychologically owning their talents. Next individuals must recognize the value derived from performing activities congruent with their talents."

Sometimes it can be a challenge to identify your strengths. You might even feel like you are not good at anything, but that is simply not true. Everyone has talents, but sometimes we get so caught up thinking about what we cannot do that we forget to think about the things we can do. Think about what you do to get that "in the zone" feeling. What do people ask you for help doing? What kind of strengths do these things require? If you are still stuck, universities often have departments with professionals who can help you explore your strengths; you might find assistance in your campus's learning center, career services, counseling, or advising departments.

Once you have explored your strengths, then it is time to put them to good use. Make them work for you. Here's an academic example: if you are in a math class and are not really good at math, but you are a great communicator, rely on the strength of communication to set up a study group, find a tutor to work with, or meet and develop a relationship with your professor. Are you suddenly going to be good at math? No, probably not. But, you will have used a strength to address a challenging area for you. It is important to remember that everybody is not good at everything. It can be frustrating to watch a friend or roommate for whom everything in school seems to come easily. Reminding yourself of your strengths can alleviate some of your frustration. Considering your strengths — being positive with yourself — and using them to your advantage, along with being aware of your weaknesses, will help you on your road to academic success.

Checkpoint

Write about a time in which you immersed yourself in learning about something just because you enjoyed it. What did you do to improve in that area? What steps did you take to get better at this skill? What did it feel like to engage in this task or activity?

_____

_____

_____

_____

_____

_____

Looking at your writing in the previous exercise, you may have realized that while engaged in the activity, you experienced **flow** — a state in which you were so immersed in an activity that time seemed to pass swiftly. You felt satisfied at every level, confident in your abilities, filled with a desire to learn and practice more. The effort involved in this activity is not taxing but rather invigorating.

How could you apply similar techniques to your academic tasks? Pick the course you are currently taking that you think will be the most challenging for you — what actions can you take to create a greater sense of flow in your academic life? What steps can you take to get better at this academic subject? What would it look and feel like to fully engage in this task or activity?

_____

_____

_____

MASLOW AND THE HIERARCHY OF NEEDS _ _ _ _ _ _ _ _ _

Psychologist Abraham Maslow (1943) theorized that people are motivated to act based on their needs. These needs are hierarchical, that is, certain needs must be met before others can be achieved. They are most often depicted as a pyramid which lists the most basic needs at the bottom and the most complicated and complex needs at the top.

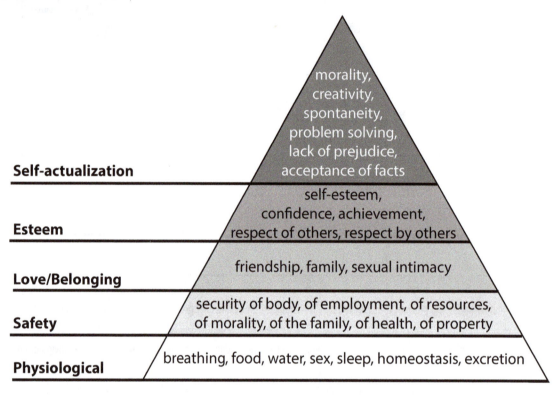

According to Maslow, an individual is able to grow and mature as needs are met; therefore, when you take care of your most basic physical and safety needs, you are then able to focus on interpersonal relationships, which then allows for an improved sense of self-esteem, which finally allows you to become, in Maslow's words "**self-actualized**" or "able to reach his potential." A key element of Maslow's theory is his assertion that you must choose which core **values** are of critical importance to achieving and maintaining full potential. That is, what are those things, characteristics, and states of being that you place the greatest importance on and that you will strive to achieve? Perhaps you have never really asked yourself that question before: "What are my values? What do I believe to be important above all other things in life?" That question deserves your full attention, so let's pull off to the side of the road and...

TAKE A REST STOP!

While it is tempting to just cruise ahead to your final destination, stopping for breaks along the way is necessary — and can be valuable for your enjoyment of the trip. The same is true in your college career: You are speeding toward graduation, but it is important to stop periodically and consider *why* you are making the trip in the first place and *how* will the trip contribute positively to your life. Here is another way to think about it: How does taking this trip tie in with the things that you believe in, the things that are important to you and will make you happier and more fulfilled as a person?

Name _____ Date _____

ACTIVITY: MAPPING MY VALUES _ _ _ _ _ _ _ _ _ _ _ _

(Indicate Yes or No for each of the categories for each value.)

Mapping My Values	Is this critically important to my well-being?	Is my life better when I feel that I possess or am in control of this?	Would I miss this if I did not have it? Do I feel like my life is less complete because I don't have this?
Creativity			
Independence			
Meaningful Relationships			
Fun and Adventure			
Respect from Others			
Power			
Financial Well-being			
Health			
Self-discipline			
Honesty			
Loyalty			

Mapping My Values	Is this critically important to my well-being?	Is my life better when I feel that I possess or am in control of this?	Would I miss this if I did not have it? Do I feel like my life is less complete because I don't have this?
Self-confidence			
Intelligence			
Job Satisfaction			
Justice			
Faith			
Leadership			
Personal Freedom			
Integrity			
Security			
Pleasure			
Service to Others			
Prestige			

For the questions you answered "yes" to, mark with a star. How many did you mark? If it is more than five, you will need to do some more thinking, because you will need to end up with the five values that matter most to you. Which of the starred values are the ones that you are going to hold close to you as you move forward in your journey? Using that criterion, select and circle the five values that you want to possess and to practice moving forward in your journey toward your goal.

Name _____   Date _____

ACTIVITY: VALUES FLOW

After you have prioritized your top five values, fill them into the Flow graphic below – make sure to articulate specifically how you plan to achieve/maintain this value in your daily life. Be specific!

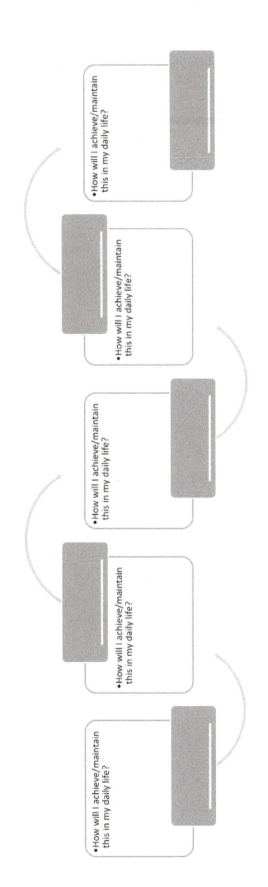

- How will I achieve/maintain this in my daily life?
- How will I achieve/maintain this in my daily life?
- How will I achieve/maintain this in my daily life?
- How will I achieve/maintain this in my daily life?
- How will I achieve/maintain this in my daily life?

WHO IS ALONG FOR THE RIDE?
By Kate Tiller

While driving alone can sometimes be relaxing and empowering, having friends along for the ride can make a long road trip much more enjoyable. A passenger on your road trip can serve as a navigator, an extra set of eyes to spot dangers ahead, and a companion to keep you awake. Having someone travel with you on your road to academic recovery will not only make the journey more enjoyable, it will also help you have someone who can hold you accountable — who can point out ideas and strategies for success you might be missing, let you know when you are not going in the right direction, and cheer with you when you succeed. Some people call this an "accountability partner."

Finding someone who you can trust to hold you accountable is the first step. You might look to a parent or older relative, or there may be a staff or faculty member on campus with whom you have developed this type of relationship. Maybe it is a roommate, friend, or sibling. The possibilities are endless. You might even find someone in your academic recovery class and work as a team to hold each other accountable.

The next step is deciding what you want that person to hold you accountable for and asking them to do so. This is why it is important to trust this person. You want to be able to talk to him about what you are trying to achieve. Telling this person the places where you struggle or have made mistakes in the past will help them to help you. Develop a plan for checking in with each other and stick to it. Having someone along for the ride will help you keep your commitments to yourself. It is important that this relationship not become one that you are totally dependent on. Remember you are ultimately responsible for your success!

SUMMARY

Are you *really* ready for a Road Trip?

Sure, you filled up and checked your tires, got your snacks and mapped your route…but how ready are *you*? Ready to enjoy the adventures — and learn from the mis-adventures — that lie ahead? Ready to engage in meaningful relationships with fellow travelers? Ready to come back from the trip a different person? A meaningful road trip is not just travel from Point A to Point B, but rather a journey, full of potholes, speed bumps, and twists and turns, and you want to be fully equipped to enjoy the ride! The work that you have been doing — examining your own habits and actions, looking forward, and defining what is important to you — will serve you well as you continue your journey in the upcoming chapters, and, indeed, on your journey to your destination: success!

Rev Your Engine

Your tank will inevitably run out of gas somewhere on this trip. What will you do to re-fuel? This journey is a long one, and you will need to think ahead to the times when your energy and enthusiasm will begin to fade. What strategies will you have available to keep you moving forward? Make a list of your go-to resources for the long stretches of highway that are a part of the journey of life:

People who inspire and support me:

Practices and habits that energize and rejuvenate me:

Books or other resources that help me see a different perspective:

CITATIONS

Downing, S. (2011). *On Course: Strategies for Creating Success in College and in Life.* Boston, MA: Wadsworth, Cengage Learning.

Duckworth, A., Peterson, C., Matthews, M.D., & Kelly, D.R. (2007). Grit: Perseverance and passion for long-term goals. *Journal of Personality and Social Psychology, 92*(4), 1087-1101.

Dweck, C.S. (2006). *Mindset: The New Psychology of Success.* New York, NY: Random House.

Hodges, T.D. and Hartner, J.K. (2005). A review of the theory and research underlying the StrengthsQuest program for students. *Educational Horizons, 83*(3), 191-201.

Maslow, A.H. (1943). A theory of human motivation. *Psychological Review, Vol 50*(4), 370-396.

Rotter, J. (1966). Generalized expectancies for internal versus external control of reinforcement. *Psychological Monographs, 80*(1), 1-28.

Ryan, R.M., & Deci, E.L. (2000). Self-determination theory and the facilitation of intrinsic motivation, social development, and well-being. *American Psychologist, 55*(1), 68-78.

Seligman, M.E.P. (2002). *Authentic Happiness: Using the New Positive Psychology to Realize Your Potential for Lasting Fulfillment.* New York, NY: Free Press.

Name _____ Date _____

Post Test/Quiz

1. What is locus of control?

2. What are the two types of motivation and how are they different?

3. True or False: The creator of the Hierarchy of Needs pyramid is Abraham Maslow.

4. What is the difference between having a fixed mindset and a growth mindset?

5. What does DAPPS stand for and what does it do?

6. True or False: Neuroplasticity of the brain is connected to a fixed mindset.

CHAPTER 3

TIME MANAGEMENT: YOUR ROAD TRIP PLANNER

By Melissa Hortman

1. LEARNING OUTCOMES: QUESTIONS TO NAVIGATE
   a. Why is it important to manage your time in college?
   b. What are different methods you could use to manage your time?
   c. How can you effectively build a calendar?
   d. What are areas in your day in which you can be more efficient in your time management?
   e. What are ways in which you can change habits so you don't procrastinate?
   f. How you can fully maximize your productivity in your scheduled time?

2. KEY CONCEPTS
   a. Methods of time management
   b. Building a calendar
   c. Planning and backdating
   d. Important versus urgent
   e. Procrastination
   f. Overcoming procrastination
   g. Aligning priorities
   h. Maximizing productivity

"You may delay, but time will not." ~ Benjamin Franklin

INTRODUCTION _____

One of the most common reasons students become academically at-risk is due to poor time management skills or simply not having any structure for their time. Time management is a skill that affects many aspects of your life, especially in college. You will want to build good time management skills now to succeed in college, have a foundation for your professional career, and be able to have a well-balanced life. Think for a moment about this road trip you are on. Do you have a destination? When do you want to get there? How many days will it take? What time do you need to get on the road each morning in order to get to your destination? The answers to these questions probably sync up with how you would answer questions about managing time in your personal life as well.

Where are you with your skills in time management and where do you want to be in terms of managing your time? Is this a skill you have struggled with in the past? Do you work too many hours at a job? Do you wait until the last minute to get work done because you'd rather hang out with friends? Are you a chronic procrastinator? Are you disorganized or have no strategy for managing your time? Consider the answer to these questions as you make your journey through this chapter.

You cannot gain more time in your journey, but you can manage the amount of time you have in an effective way. Have you ever thought about how some people manage to get so much done in one day? Every person is given the same amount of time in the day; it is what you, as an individual, do with your time that matters. Students manage their time differently, such as to-do lists, online calendars, sticky notes, daily planners, or semester calendars. You may prefer to look at the "big picture" because the details give you anxiety, or you may like the hour-by-hour calendar to know exactly what you need to get done because you are so busy. No one way is the right way to manage your time but you do have to pick some way. In this chapter, you will be exposed to several options to help you begin to manage your time more effectively.

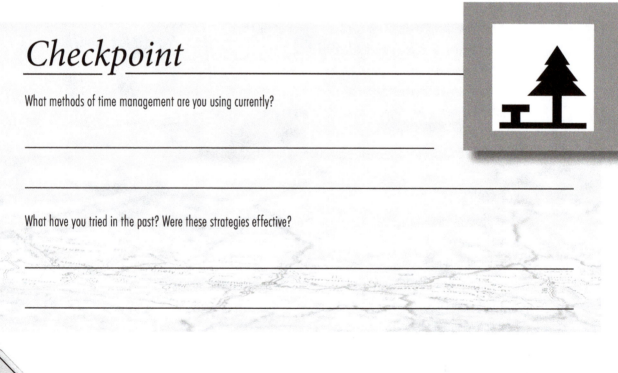

Checkpoint _____

What methods of time management are you using currently?

_____

_____

What have you tried in the past? Were these strategies effective?

_____

_____

As you find a strategy to manage your time, whether it is through traditional or technological methods, be sure to commit to it and stick with it and make this part of your life. It takes 30 days to develop a habit, so choose a method and give it 30 days of consciously integrating it into your day to see if it is something you want to continue.

METHODS OF TIME MANAGEMENT

There are many different **methods of time management** you can use throughout your journey, and listed below are a few options with positive and negative views of each. First, you need to consider what level of involvement and time frame you want to manage: daily to-do lists, weekly, monthly, or view the whole semester?

To-do lists are great small checklists for students who want a task-specific list they can follow and not be restricted to time. This kind of empowerment, as you cross tasks off your list, and freedom, where you are not tied to a time deadline throughout your day, makes to-do lists a very good option for a lot of people. One hint to making your to-do list effective is to be very specific in the task you need to complete. For example, do not write down, "Do biology homework"; instead write, "Complete Chapters 1-3 in Biology Textbook; finish problems 1-10 at the end of each chapter; and submit online by midnight." The more specific the goal, the more likely you are going to be able to complete it. Remember to limit the size of your to-do list by identifying three to four key things you must accomplish each day. As you complete all of the tasks on your daily to-do list, you should throw it away. This way you cannot just transfer tasks to the next day and the next. Usually students will use some sort of calendar method and a to-do list to supplement the bigger picture with more of the details.

Weekly calendars are a very popular time management choice. These calendars can either be broken up into time segments or full days. This strategy gives you more control over the day and allows for the integration of the bigger picture of the week. Knowing what is coming up and being able to plan out your day when you are very busy are some of the most effective ways of managing your time, and you can use both of those skills in a weekly calendar. Weekly calendars can be found online (so you can print them out), in planners, on wall calendars, and many more places. Find a weekly calendar that fits your needs. In the next section you will do an activity based on a weekly calendar to see how this time management method works for you.

Monthly calendars are good for those that like to see the bigger picture, who may not need all the details, and who like to have a plan. Imagine creating a monthly calendar that included all of the tasks from each of your syllabi on it. A monthly calendar can help you to plan out your weeks and weekends with all that you have coming up. Monthly calendars can be found in many forms, such as desk calendars, wall calendars, monthly planner, or month-at-a-glance on a sheet of paper you can create and print out.

Semester calendars. Having all the weeks of the semester laid out so you can see them all at one time can help you to plan the big events happening throughout your semester, such as papers, exams, or assignments. If you complete this at the beginning of the semester, you can start to see busy weeks of the semester and plan ahead for them. Check online or with your campus to see if they have semester-at-a-glance academic calendars available for you to use or consider creating one yourself.

FORMATS OF TIME MANAGEMENT

Now it's time to consider the format you want to keep: electronic and mobile or paper?

Electronic Calendars and Mobile Apps. Electronic calendars are a very popular method for managing time. With phones and technology always on and accessible, you can send yourself reminders, quickly update and add events, and check in on your schedule, to keep on task. From re-occurring events to filling in all the details you need, electronic calendars can simplify the calendar experience with some work on the front end to set it up. There are many options when it comes to electronic calendars, so do some research before committing to this format.

Using electronic calendars is not for everyone. Since it is not a physical calendar, you do not have it out with you all the time, and you cannot physically write in it. Be aware if you need to write tasks out to remember them or if you can simply put it in an online calendar to remind yourself before the event. If you do not access your technology often, online calendars may not be the best idea for you.

Mobile devices are upgrading all of the time to give you better applications and accessibility to time management software. There is a new app being created every day and with thousands of apps to choose from already, your options are almost unlimited. Since mobile devices are with you at all times, this is an easy way to integrate a time management method into your life. Whether it is a to-do list app or timer, you can find an app that can enhance and probably improve the efficiency of what you are already doing. Know that technology has a rigid structure in its design and often a lot of back end work needs to be done before you can fully enjoy an app. Be sure to do your research first and read the reviews so you do not waste a lot of your time setting up an app that you might not like or use after a week.

Paper Planners come in all shapes and sizes, with pages that may cover one day or three days, days broken down by hour or just a single box to fill in, as large as a binder or small enough to fit in your pocket. Be sure to invest in a planner that fits your needs and the way you like to plan. Having a planner is great to have in class when the professor tells you what to do for homework or if they change the date of an assignment. Choose to keep the planner open on your desk during class to add, change, or edit any assignments or tasks you need to complete before the next class or exam. Invest in a bookmark or binder clip to keep the day or week clipped so you can turn right to it. Make using a planner as easy as possible for you as a time management method.

As you are planning your road trip, remember, it would be best to use a maximum of one or two methods. If you are using more than two methods, it will be hard to keep up with the management of the calendars. Try to decide on using one detail-oriented planning method and one bigger-picture planning method. For example, you could plan on using sticky notes for small to-do lists and the semester calendar to see the whole semester at a glance.

Name _____ Date _____

ACTIVITY: WHERE DOES YOUR TIME GO? _ _ _ _ _ _ _ _ _

Everyone starts the week with the same number of hours. So, why does your time go so fast? Let's find out!

Number of hours of sleep each night   _____ x 7 = _____

Number of hours spent grooming each day   _____ x 7 = _____

Number of hours for meals/snacks
(including preparation/clean-up time)   _____ x 7 = _____

Travel time to and from campus   _____ x _____ = _____

Number of hours per week for regular activities
(volunteer work, intramurals, church, clubs, etc.)   = _____

Number of hours per day of errands, etc.   _____ x 7 = _____

Number of hours of work per week   = _____

Number of hours of class per week   = _____

Number of hours per week with friends,
social parties, going out, etc.   = _____

Number of hours of TV and computer   _____ x 7 = _____

Total = _____

168.0 hours in a week

- _____ hours of activities

= _____ hours to study

    These estimations allow you to calculate the approximate amount of time you have to study during the week. Is there enough time? You may need to look at how to reorganize your time to allow for more/less study time each week.

GETTING ORGANIZED!
By Kate Tiller

Getting yourself organized can make a long road trip go more smoothly. On your road to academic recovery, getting yourself organized will help you put all the strategies you are learning into practice. Organization is more than just using a calendaring system, although that is a very important habit to develop. Organizing your study space and your study materials can help you, especially during those crazy and stressful times throughout the semester.

First, think about where you study and where you keep your academic materials. If you study at home or in your residence hall room, try to create a designated space that is relatively quiet. Make sure you have enough room to be able to spread out your various materials. If you have a computer or a laptop, make sure there is additional desktop space. Make sure you have sufficient light. Place other things you need like pencils, pens, highlighters, paper, notecards, etc. nearby so you do not to have to search for them before you start to study.

If you study at the library, a local coffee shop, outside in the sunshine...or anywhere you are any time you get a spare minute, you can also organize yourself so that you can study on the move. Pack a bag that has those must-haves for studying. Having a few pens and pencils, a highlighter, a pack of notecards, an extra charger, and maybe a snack and a bottle of water packed in a bag allows you to simply add relevant books and be ready to study at a moment's notice. You will not waste time finding materials you need to start your study session.

Beyond your study space, having a system to organize your lecture notes (if you do not take notes electronically) and handouts will help you be more efficient with your time. Different systems work for different people, and there is no wrong way to organize as long as it works for you. You could take one large binder and use a divider for each class. Dividers with pockets allow you to quickly put handouts in the right section. Later, you can punch holes in those handouts and slide them into the binder. You can follow the same concept with a slimmer binder for each class or use medium-sized binders for classes that meet on the same day of the week. Some students prefer spiral notebooks. Choosing a large notebook with divided sections that have pockets or several spiral notebooks with pockets will help you keep up with those extra handouts you get. If you prefer a composition book, legal pad, or electronic device for note taking, having a slim pocketed folder for each class is a necessity.

Again, there is no right or wrong method for organization. Having a system in place that you get into the habit of using will help you when you run into speed bumps along the way. When school is stressful — you have three tests, a paper, and a presentation in the same week — already being organized will allow for things to go more smoothly.

Name _____ Date _____

ACTIVITY: WEEKLY CALENDAR – WRITE IT DOWN AS YOU GO

Do you know where all of your time goes each day? Do you know if you use your time effectively? Use the first weekly calendar, which is broken down in hour increments, to write down what you are doing with your time as it passes. You are not scheduling ahead what you are going to do, but rather documenting what you have just done throughout the hours in your day. Fill in each hour block with the specific activity you are doing. For example, if you watched a movie for three hours in the afternoon, be sure to put that on your time log, or if you woke up at 1:00 p.m. on Saturday, be sure write that down, or if you sat in the library but did not really study till 10:00 p.m., write that down. Be honest in this activity, as it will help you to see how you are spending your time!

Without even knowing it, you will start to see certain things in your day taking up a lot of your time, as well as times of day when you are not being productive. Go back and highlight those things that you think are wasting your time on the first calendar you completed.

1. Put an asterisk (*) by those leisure activities. Do you need to cut things out of your day so more work can be done?
2. Add up how many hours you studied. How many should you have studied (2 hours for every hour in class)? _____
3. How many did you actually study? _____

Write it Down as You Go! Calendar

	Mon.	Tues.	Wed.	Thurs.	Fri.	Sat.	Sun.
7 am							
8 am							
9 am							
10 am							
11 am							
Noon							
1 pm							
2 pm							
3 pm							
4 pm							
5 pm							
6 pm							
7 pm							
8 pm							
9 pm							
10 pm							
11 pm							
Midnight							

ACTIVITY: WEEKLY CALENDAR – BUILDING YOUR SCHEDULE

Do you know what your non-negotiable obligations are each day of the week? Do you know where to fit in "everything else" that needs to be done? Use the second weekly calendar that is broken down in hour increments to **build your calendar** for the week ahead. With this calendar we will be looking forward and planning out the tasks you are scheduled to do and tasks you would like to do each day.

First, you will want to block off all of your non-negotiables: these are tasks such as classes, eating, sleeping, studying, work, and any weekly meetings or activities you are required to attend. Block your classes off first; if you are a full time student, you will be in class for 12-20 hours a week (as much time as a part time job) and studying an additional 24-40 hours a week. Experts say you should be studying two to three hours outside of class for every hour you are in class; this is so you have time to rewrite-notes, read for class, do assignments, keep up with discussions, and take time to learn material and not just memorize it. Studying should then be a non-negotiable. This in turn, makes being a full time student equivalent to working a full time job. Think about this as you fill in the rest of your non-negotiables. Eating breakfast, lunch, and dinner must be on your calendar at reasonable times to keep your energy up for all that you have to do throughout your day and the length of time you leave for eating is up to you. Be sure to put a cut-off time at night to be able to get 6 to 10 hours of sleep each night. Add in work, meetings, or activities since these are tasks you have decided to be obligated to. Your week should look a lot less open.

Now, you will want to add in any additional tasks or events you may want to have on your calendar so you are sure to make time for them. This can be a personal errand, going to an event on campus, making time for the beach or friends, scheduled time to exercise throughout your week, or simply having time for you. These tasks may change from day-to-day and week-to-week, which will allow for flexibility in how you choose what is important enough to put on your calendar and make time for. Remember "time suckers" like getting ready in the morning or at night, cooking your food, walking to the dining hall, stopping to talk to friends, walking to class, and watching TV or movies. Plan buffer time for these activities that could take more or less time than you originally planned. Try to stick to the calendar you have planned for this coming week.

Building Your Schedule Calendar

	Mon.	Tues.	Wed.	Thurs.	Fri.	Sat.	Sun.
7 am							
8 am							
9 am							
10 am							
11 am							
Noon							
1 pm							
2 pm							
3 pm							
4 pm							
5 pm							
6 pm							
7 pm							
8 pm							
9 pm							
10 pm							
11 pm							
Midnight							

Scenic Overlook

Once you get through the week, assess to see how you can make your calendar work better for the next week. Use the backside of the weekly calendar to plan your next week. Does anything look different on your calendar this second time around? How will you plan your week differently? You should go through this process every week at the beginning of the week to be sure you are becoming more and more efficient in building your schedule. Use this schedule for one more week to see if you can make any more changes to be even more efficient in your time.

Name _____ Date _____

PLANNING CALENDAR

	Mon.	Tues.	Wed.	Thurs.	Fri.	Sat.	Sun.
7 am							
8 am							
9 am							
10 am							
11 am							
Noon							
1 pm							
2 pm							
3 pm							
4 pm							
5 pm							
6 pm							
7 pm							
8 pm							
9 pm							
10 pm							
11 pm							
Midnight							

Scenic Overlook —————

Were you effective with the use of your time or were you just efficient in the tasks you completed? Did you do the right things to meet your personal goals? How can you schedule your time each week so you maintain a balance, as well as meet your responsibilities? How will creating and following a prioritized schedule help you?

PLANNING ——————————————————————

No one plans to fail, they just fail to plan.

Taking time to plan is one of the most important steps of time management. If you have a calendar that is not useful to you with information on it that you don't follow, then there is no use in having it. In this section, you will learn how to decipher between what is **important versus urgent.** Steven Covey's time management matrix can help you look at your tasks in a different light to understand where they fall in the spectrum of urgent and important to you and how you can then prioritize them.

Do you know what is urgent and important in your life?

Take a moment to look at Steven Covey's time management matrix to help you differentiate between tasks that are urgent, not urgent, important, and not important in your life. You want to be spending the majority of your time in Quadrant II, where activities are important but not urgent.

	URGENT	**NOT URGENT**
IMPORTANT	*Quadrant I:* Urgent & Important	*Quadrant II:* Not Urgent & Important
NOT IMPORTANT	*Quadrant III:* Urgent & Not Important	*Quadrant IV:* Not Urgent & Not Important

Source: Stephen Covey, *7 Habits of Highly Effective People*

You can start to see how tasks on your road trip can be categorized into the different quadrants above. Now, take a moment to fill out the matrix below with tasks on your to-do list right now to see where they fall. Is your matrix overloaded in one section? What tasks are you avoiding and do you have good reason to be avoiding them?

MY MATRIX

	URGENT	NOT URGENT
IMPORTANT	I	II
NOT IMPORTANT	III	IV

Scenic Overlook

When you can start to figure out what is important and not urgent in your life, you can sort what you value and what you need to accomplish first. Continue to use a matrix like this as you get new tasks on your list and are not sure of how to prioritize them on your calendar. Remember when what is important to you aligns with what you need to get done, you can maximize your productivity!

BACKDATING

Backdating is a very important concept when planning and scheduling, as it can help you break down assignments and tests into manageable pieces that you can schedule on your calendar. Think of **planning and backdating** as breaking up the project and scheduling each of the pieces to be done at a different point, building on the last piece, leading up to the final project being due. If you know your destination, be sure you plan the best route possible to get there in the most efficient way possible. Professors often give you the due dates of assignments and tests in their course. Although it is good to see when that final date is on your calendar, it is also good to backdate those assignments and tests to be sure you can break down each of the pieces that need to be completed and complete them well. This can make an assignment less overwhelming by having each of the pieces laid out ahead of time, and a test less stressful because you have studied different sections leading up to the test. Do you have a term paper due this semester? Try out "backdating" on the schedule, starting with when the paper is due and working backwards.

Name _____ Date _____

ACTIVITY: BACKDATING A PAPER _ _ _ _ _ _ _ _ _ _ _ _ _ _

To Do	Energy Types	How	Date Due
Identify your topic	Creative	Note what interests you in lectures, readings, and in conversations.	
Search for sources	Creative	Spend time in the library and in databases to collect information via notecards, electronically, or on paper to be able to shuffle through and brainstorm.	
Know the documentation style	Critical	Find out the documentation style of the paper. If you need to know how to use it, visit a librarian or your learning assistance center to get information on how to write in that style.	
Narrow your topic	Critical	This can be done while you are doing research on your topic. Is there enough research on your topic? If not, make necessary changes.	
Write thesis statement and supporting points to create a working outline	Creative	Write your thesis statement to guide your paper and begin pulling out supporting points from your research. Show your main ideas, major details, and minor details.	
Write rough draft, using your outline	Creative	Does your thesis need to be revised or refined as you begin your rough draft? Your learning assistance center can help — sometimes it is just starting that is the hardest.	
Develop a works cited sheet	Critical	Always keep track of all the sources you are using for your entire paper.	
Allow time to be objective	Patience		At least 24 hours
Take a rough draft to your tutoring lab for revision	Critical	Check for unity, paragraph organization, rethink major issues. Make sure your conclusion matches your thesis. Have a roommate, friend, or professor sit down on a one-on-one basis and revise your paper with you.	
Revise paper, based on comments	Critical	Hopefully a few people were able to look at your paper and give you comments and edits. If needed, take another draft to a professor or your learning assistance center.	
Allow time to be objective	Patience		At least 24 hours
Proofread for edits	Critical	Check sentence structure, word choice, grammar, and citations. Read your paper out loud making sure it doesn't sound awkward.	
Complete draft and submit	Critical	Do one final read-over to be sure you followed directions and completed the objective of the paper. Finally, submit your paper!	

PROCRASTINATION: SPEED BUMPS AHEAD _____

Riddle me this: What is the longest and yet the shortest thing in the world? The swiftest and yet the slowest, the most divisible and the most extended, the least valued and the most regretted, without which nothing can be done, which devours everything, however small, and yet opens the life and spirit, to every object, however great? – Phil Cousineau

What do you think the answer to the riddle is? The answer to the riddle is time! Now that you know the answer, go back and read the riddle again with time in mind as the answer to all of the questions. **Procrastination** is a setback in time everyone has experienced at some point or another. Some are minor cases, like putting off going to the grocery store until nighttime because you don't want to drive on crowded roads during the day; and some are much more severe cases, like putting off writing a paper until hours before it is due because you simply do not like writing. Imagine packing minutes before you leave on a trip; it is confusing, hectic, and you are probably going to forget some important things. In some cases it is not always terrible to procrastinate; however, when you are given a deadline for schoolwork or projects for your job, procrastination can debilitate you and your success. Most procrastinators already know what they need to accomplish, yet they continually tell themselves they can put it off until later because maybe they will be more motivated, or they will just push through the task, or they work better under pressure, or they know they can "knock it out" in just a few hours.

Every student finds their own excuse to procrastinate and their own way of making up for the lost time while procrastinating. Think about a time when you procrastinated. Why did you procrastinate on the task? What did you do while procrastinating on a task — a "time waster" activity? How long did you procrastinate as the deadline approached? Throughout this section your thinking will be challenged on procrastination and hopefully you will have a better idea of how to answer these questions.

Checkpoint

Imagine you are going to get $86,400 today and you have to spend all of the money today. You cannot save it in the bank or put it in stock. You must spend all of the money. What would you spend the money on? Write down a few of them below.

_____

_____

_____

86,400 is a very exact number for a reason. It is the amount of seconds we have in each day. You probably chose to spend your money on things that meant something to you, maybe large or small. This is how you should be planning your day. When you are procrastinating, you are throwing away one dollar for every second. If you think about your time as money, you might not waste so much of it.

WHAT MAKES YOU PROCRASTINATE? _ _ _ _ _ _ _ _ _

Checkpoint

Take a moment to think about a task or assignment that you have been procrastinating on. Whether the task is large or small, you may be putting off doing the task for one reason or another. Go through using the different prompts provided and identify your reasons for delaying the task as stated below.

Reasons for Delay (controlling influences)

1._____

2._____

Procrastination Activities (what you would rather be doing)

1._____

2._____

Positive Consequences of Procrastination (why it feels/is good to delay)

1._____

2._____

Arguments Against Delay (convince yourself why not to delay)

1._____

2._____

Negative Consequences of Procrastination (why you shouldn't delay)

1._____

2._____

Did it help to go through this process to figure out ways around not procrastinating on a certain task? What are the next steps for you? As you find yourself putting tasks off, take time to answer these questions to see why you may be doing this. Look for trends that may emerge to help you figure out what makes you procrastinate and the reasons for it!

Scenic Overlook

What interruptions and time-wasters do you encounter? Everyone has them. How can you avoid these time intrusions? When you catch yourself doing them can you ask yourself, "What's the best use of my time right now?"

REASONS STUDENTS PROCRASTINATE

Every student has their reasons for procrastinating; some are just more recognizable than others. You may not even know yet what those reasons are or maybe you are starting to recognize trends from the last activity. Ultimately the first step is to recognize self-defeating problems such as fear and anxiety, difficulty concentrating, poor time management, indecisiveness, or perfectionism. The following are the most popular reasons that students procrastinate. As you go through each of the reasons, think about how this trait could relate to you.

Poor time management – Not every student coming to college is coming with everything figured out. Even after some time in college, you may not have all of the kinks worked out in your planning. This is not a terrible thing; it is normal not to have it all figured out. You will grow these skills as you progress along your educational journey with trial and error leading your decision-making. As you try out new methods of time management that may or may not be working for you, it will take a lot of extra time and effort. This may lead to procrastination because you are not at your most efficient level of time management. One quick tip to combat procrastination would be to choose one method of time management and make a conscious effort to stick with it for a month so you can get used to it while pushing yourself to not procrastinate. You are bettering your skills while also pushing yourself to avoid procrastination!

Difficulty concentrating – Concentration on schoolwork is difficult with so many distractions along your road trip. With your days filled with class, hanging out with friends, errands, and many other things to keep you occupied, there is little time left to sit and concentrate on schoolwork. Distractions even spill over into the nighttime so it becomes just as difficult to concentrate. Maybe it's not the distractions as much as you're tired from being so busy all day, you have many other things on your mind, there are problems at home, or you have a hard time sitting and concentrating on a particular subject. One quick tip to combat difficulty concentrating is to study in small blocks of time instead of long time periods. For example, you will accomplish more if you study in 60-minute blocks and take frequent 10-minute breaks in between, than if you study for 2-3 hours straight with no breaks. These are called "power hours" and can be really useful because you set a purpose for studying, complete your studying, take a break, and then check in with yourself to see if you accomplished your purpose. This is better than aimless hours of "reading."

THE POWER HOURS OF STUDYING _____

2-5 minutes	Set Your Purpose	What do you need to accomplish? Are there questions you should be able to answer at the end?
40 minutes	Study	
10 minutes	Take a break	Walk, get a snack/drink, check social media (with a timer)
10 minutes	Check Your Purpose	Did you meet your goal for this power hour? If not, try again. If so, then move on!

Fear and anxiety –It can be debilitating when fear and anxiety affects schoolwork. When you constantly have anxiety about starting, completing, or turning in an assignment, it is natural then to put it off for as long as possible so you will not have to feel that anxiety. These emotions can be conscious, where you know what emotion is inhibiting you from doing your work; or unconscious, where you don't know what is keeping you from doing your work. One quick way to combat this is to keep a journal of how you are feeling when you procrastinate. Are you anxious about the amount of work that needs to be done? Are you fearful of how studying for a test may turn out? Writing down these emotions can help you to figure out what those emotions are, whether they are fear or anxiety, and help you seek help and move on.

Negative beliefs and attitude – Having a negative attitude about an assignment can set you back more than you know. It can unconsciously turn you off from an assignment that you could have knocked out in less time than thinking negatively about it. When negative beliefs and attitudes spill over into your academic tasks, you have a very high chance of procrastinating until that emotion or thought is gone. One quick tip to combat a negative attitude is, even if you are not fully sure of the assignment, get started on something. You may forget that you had a negative attitude about a task while you are accomplishing it!

Finding the task boring – Not every assignment in every class is going to be the most interesting task you have ever completed. Although finding a task boring may be expected at some point in your college career, you also need to know how to push through this feeling. Make it a competition to complete the task: compete with yourself, set a timer so you only spend 30 minutes a day on the task, write one interesting thing about the task, or talk to the professor to see if you can change the assignment to include something you are more interested in. There are a lot of options besides procrastinating on a task because you find it boring. One quick tip would be to motivate yourself to study by dwelling on success and not on failure. Rewarding yourself after you complete a task could help you overcome your procrastination habits so they do not impede upon completing an assignment. For example, if you like to watch movies, save this for when you complete a task so it becomes a reward.

Unrealistic expectations – If you think you can write a 10-page paper in 3 hours, you have set unrealistic expectations for yourself. These unrealistic expectations can get you into trouble when you underestimate the amount of time you will need to spend on an assignment. Start out early to see how long tasks are taking you. Set a timer when you sit to write a paper to see how long it takes to write a page or when you sit to read a certain course's textbook and see how long it takes to read a page. This way you are starting to build a real time schedule for yourself so you can be realistic in your planning and specific in your goals for tasks. For example, "read and outline chapter 10" or "read for 20 minutes, then write a short summary," as opposed to "read for history class."

All of these reasons for procrastinating are legitimate as well as debilitating to your goal of reaching your destination. However, each reason has multiple ways in which you can combat procrastination. Once you recognize your reasons for procrastination and quick ways in which you can overcome them, you can then move on to identifying your own goals, strengths, weaknesses, values, and priorities. When your goals and values align with how you are using your time, you will be much more efficient and waste less time procrastinating.

WHAT DO YOU DO WHEN YOU PROCRASTINATE? _ _ _ _ _

Students all have their own way of procrastinating, ranging from sleeping to watching movies. Some students even do other work instead of the work that needs to be done — this is called "productive avoidance." Do you know what you are doing when you procrastinate? One way to keep track of this would be with a "shame journal." This means literally writing all of the things you did as you procrastinated in a journal every day. Keep this journal for a month and look back to see what your trends are and what vices you need to avoid. Knowing what you are doing instead of doing your work can help you restructure your day so you can still do these things but they do not get in the way of the tasks you need to complete for your classes.

Most of the time procrastination happens when you put yourself in a certain environment — in your residence hall room, with your friends, or off campus. Modify your environment to eliminate or minimize noises and distractions. Ensure you have adequate lighting when studying so you are not making your eyes work twice as hard and getting tired faster. You should have all the necessary equipment at hand so you don't waste time going back and forth to get things. Don't get too comfortable when studying: a desk and straight-backed chair are usually best. A bed is no place to study! If you can, be neat! Take a few minutes to straighten your workspace because this can help to reduce day-dreaming. Setting up the right environment can keep you from procrastinating and make you more efficient when studying!

Checkpoint

In the boxes below, you will see "when you hear yourself saying... you can make a change by..." to help you work through some scenarios that may be familiar to you as you **overcome procrastination**. Take some time with each of the boxes on the right to write in your own strategy to make a change for each of the different sayings.

When you hear yourself saying...	You can make a change by...
"I turned it in late because I needed more information/ wasn't sure it was right/wanted to wait until I had a really good idea."	❑ Starting the next project earlier ❑ Making a timetable of tasks ❑ Asking for clarification of assignment right away, so you don't "second-guess" yourself later ❑ Reminding yourself that you have the ability to do a good job ❑ _____
"I didn't have enough time to study for it, so I got a bad grade."	❑ Asking yourself why you didn't make the time, if doing well on the test was a priority for you ❑ Figuring out what you did during that time, if you weren't studying ❑ Looking ahead on the syllabus to check the date of the next test, then creating a regular study schedule to cover the material ❑ _____
"I meant to do that this weekend."	❑ Realizing that good intentions mean very little; you need to take action to make something happen ❑ Realizing that you tend to put off things that you don't want to do; could you have done it first to get it out of the way? ❑ Making a short list of things that you need to do during the weekend ❑ _____
"I didn't get it done because my friend was having a crisis and really needed me."	❑ Not allowing yourself to be sabotaged; your friends are important, but school is your top priority ❑ Being honest: Were you looking for a reason to avoid the task? ❑ _____
"I didn't get it done because I always wait until the last minute and I don't know how to break the cycle."	❑ Make a recurring appointment with an academic coach on your campus ❑ Realizing that you procrastinate and want to do something about it ❑ _____
_____ _____ _____ _____	❑ _____ ❑ _____ ❑ _____ ❑ _____

Hopefully you have seen that there are a lot of ways to look back on the excuses you may have made because you procrastinated and turn them into opportunities to grow and change. Don't be discouraged if you fall back into your procrastination habits, just recognize them and continue to push for change next time. If you hear yourself saying something frequently, refer back to this section and add your own strategies for change.

MAXIMIZING YOUR PRODUCTIVITY _ _ _ _ _ _ _ _ _ _

There are a lot of challenges to being productive! Do you relate to any of these?

o   Maintaining motivation
o   Disciplining yourself to schedule and complete tasks
o   Keeping up morale each day with what you need to accomplish
o   Putting off doing something
o   "Relaxing" too much on the weekends or during breaks
o   Feeling overwhelmed by the daunting tasks ahead
o   Resisting distractions in the form of a roommate or technology
o   Feeling pressure from yourself or others to get tasks done and doing them well
o   Managing stress or anxiety that try to inhibit your academic success
o   Overcoming unhealthy habits that are challenging you

If you do relate to any of the previous statements, think of finding a way to overcome that challenge so as to **maximize your productivity**. It may mean only changing one feeling, emotion, or task in your day to allow you to enhance how you are managing your time.

Checkpoint

Do you know what the best times of your day are to be effective and study? Be aware of how your emotions affect you during your day. You may be groggy in the morning, anxious in the afternoon, or not able to concentrate at night. Know your schedule and how your classes and study time can fit into that schedule. Do not try to alter your emotional schedule to fit your life; it takes a lot of time and effort to change your emotional schedule. Be honest with yourself and what is going on so you are not working against your body and brain! It would be like getting up at 5:00 a.m. every morning when you know you are not a morning person.

MANAGING IT ALL
By Kate Tiller

Think about all of the things people try to do while they are driving: texting, eating, applying makeup, and talking on the phone. Multitasking while driving can lead to very dangerous outcomes. However, multitasking is an essential part of a college student's world. Maybe you work full time, have a family, care for a relative, lead a campus organization, or participate in college athletics.

Perhaps you fall into more than one of those categories. Many students have commitments that make truly focusing on their academic success difficult. If this is true for you, one of the first things you must do is PRIORITIZE. List the commitments, the things in your life for which you are responsible, in 1-2-3 order in the first box. Then in the second box, list the top five values you identified in the Mapping My Values exercise in the first chapter. Finally, draw a line connecting each of your commitments to the value that they fulfill. This exercise will give you the chance to reflect on the relationship between your values and your commitments outside of school.

List your five values from the Mapping My Values exercise:

1.

2.

3.

4.

5.

List your commitments here:

_____

_____

_____

_____

_____

If you have commitments that do not align with your values, consider what that means about those commitments. Is there anything that you can eliminate from your life? Sometimes you have to say NO to certain things so that you can say YES to the things that really matter. Also consider the role school plays in this picture. If you are a student-athlete, for example, you know that your academic recovery is directly connected to your athletic eligibility. If your goal is to earn your college degree so that you can better support your family, your commitment to school is important to your family's future. Sometimes you have to realign your priorities in order to ultimately meet all of your responsibilities.

If your commitments seem to align with your values and/or you cannot step away from any of your responsibilities for even a semester, you have to figure out how to use your time as efficiently and effectively as possible. In this chapter you are learning some specific strategies that will help you improve time management skills. You will have the opportunity to learn new strategies for note-taking, reading, organization, and time management. Using these strategies will allow you to be more efficient as you meet your academic responsibilities as well as your personal ones. By applying these strategies, the multitasking required on your life's journey will be more manageable.

Sometimes, however, students find themselves so lost and overwhelmed that they need to pull over and reroute their academic and career paths. If that is you, you might want to consider taking some time off from school. Some schools have leave-of-absence options for students who are dealing with significant life events. Or, even if there is not a formal leave of absence process or if you do not qualify for a leave of absence, there is often a path for reentry for a student who completes a full withdrawal from the institution. **Of course, the policies and procedures for these types of options are different at every school. Check with your campus to find out your options.**

SUMMARY

You read in this chapter how valuable time and self-management are to your journey through college and ultimately reaching your destination. As you make decisions on how to manage your time, think about how this method would work in a professional career. Managing your time does not stop after college — it continues for the rest of your life. College is a good time to test out different methods and ways of overcoming barriers and challenges to time management. You may never be perfect at managing your time, but becoming more efficient with your time is the main goal. There are many ways to improve your time management skills, but making these new skills a habit is the important destination as you travel your journey.

Rev Your Engine

30 Day Challenge with 30 Time Savers

Challenge yourself to implement one of these time savers each day for the next 30 days and maximize your productivity along the way!

1. Set priorities for tasks — most important to least important.
2. Fight procrastination! If it is a priority, do it now!
3. Subdivide large tasks into smaller ones.
4. Establish an hour or half hour to focus.
5. Find a hideaway spot to study.
6. Learn to say "no" to avoid overbooking yourself.
7. Learn to delegate when working in groups.
8. Accumulate similar tasks and do them together.
9. Limit your time checking email or social media.
10. Perfectionism can't always be the goal.
11. An active body and healthier meals lead to a sharper mind.
12. Get enough sleep to have your mind well rested to be productive.
13. Reward yourself when you are done with a task whether large or small!
14. Utilize technology to your advantage.
15. Schedule everything — even time for classes, studying, eating, and relaxing!
16. Don't over-schedule yourself. Allow for downtime and unexpected situations.
17. Set time limits for tasks.
18. Concentrate on the task at hand.
19. Do difficult tasks first.
20. Think and plan the task before doing it.
21. Do a task thoroughly before moving on: do it right the first time!
22. Use a highly visible wall calendar or time management technique in addition to/instead of a planner.
23. Study smarter, not harder: study groups, tutors, etc.

24. Use small periods of day time in between classes.
25. Use your energy cycles to find times in the day when you are most alert.
26. Seek out academic support opportunities.
27. Put away all distractions.
28. Avoid "efficiency traps" — being efficient doesn't always mean you are productive.
29. Clean your desk or desktop before attempting to concentrate.
30. Find a role model or mentor to keep you accountable.

CITATIONS

Britton, B., & Tesser, A. (1991). Effects of time-management practices on college grades. *Journal of Educational Psychology, (83)* 3, 405-410.

Covey, S., Merrill, A., & Merrill, R. (1994*). First Things First: To Love, To Learn, To Leave a Legacy.* New York, NY: Simon and Schuster.

Hoffman, E. (2011). Maslow and Management Theory. *The Peak Experience.* Retrieved from *Learn to Leave a Legacy.* New York, NY: Simon and Schuster.

Marano, H.E. (2010). Procrastination: Ten Things to Know. Retrieved from http://www.psychologytoday.com/articles/200308/procrastination-ten-things-know

Zeenath, S., & Orcullo, D.J. (2012). Exploring academic procrastination among undergraduates. *International Proceedings of Economics Development & Research, (47)*, 42.

POST TEST/QUIZ

1. How many days does it take to develop a habit?

2. Name the 4 areas of Steven Covey's Time Management Matrix and your key to action for each.

3. What is backdating in planning?

4. What is the first thing you should put on your weekly calendar when building it?

5. Name 5 time management methods.

6. What 3 things does Maslow's hierarchy in time management teach you to not let other tasks intrude on what is essential in your life?

7. What are 5 time savers you can try?

8. What are 2 reasons students procrastinate?

9. When you hear yourself saying, "I meant to do that this weekend," what are 2 things you can do to make a change?

10. What 2 areas of your life need to match up to schedule and use your time more efficiently?

11. From your own personal experience, list three time-management tips.

CHAPTER 4

READING THE MAP TO GUIDE YOURSELF

By Melissa Thomas

1. **LEARNING OUTCOMES: QUESTIONS TO NAVIGATE**
   a. What is critical thinking?
   b. Why read in college?
   c. How do you tackle different texts differently? Math textbook? Online readings?
   d. What speed bumps will get in the way of you completing your readings?
   e. What are active reading strategies?
   f. How can you manage your readings and your time?

2. **KEY CONCEPTS**
   a. Reading
   b. Critical thinking
   c. Executive functioning
   d. Metacognition
   e. Reading rate
   f. Active versus passive reading strategies

This chapter starts a series of chapters that all relate to academic success: the skills and strategies that can equate to success inside the classroom. These skills build upon one another and start with the foundation of reading.

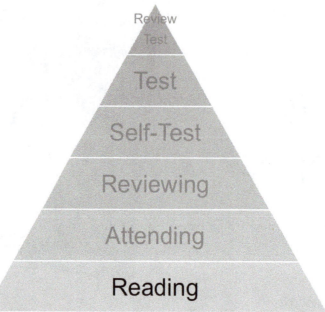

INTRODUCTION ------------------------------

What is reading? **Reading** is making meaning from text (decoding and encoding information). People decode information in order to understand what someone is trying to convey and encode information in order to explain that information to themselves or others. Decoding and encoding involve critically thinking about information as it comes in and out of our minds. What worked (or didn't work) before probably won't work for you now. College-level reading skills involve critical thinking and active reading. So what does a critical thinker look like?

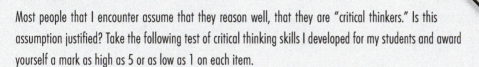

ARE YOU A CRITICAL THINKER?

Dr. Thomas A. Shipka,
Philosophy and Religious Studies, Youngstown State University
Youngstown, OH

Most people that I encounter assume that they reason well, that they are "critical thinkers." Is this assumption justified? Take the following test of critical thinking skills I developed for my students and award yourself a mark as high as 5 or as low as 1 on each item.

_____ I am a successful problem-solver.

_____ I am an informed and responsible decision-maker. I gather as many relevant facts as time constraints permit and I anticipate the likely consequences of each option before I make a decision.

_____ I strive for informed beliefs, that is, beliefs based on compelling evidence and strong arguments.

_____ I use language with precision and clarity.

_____ My beliefs are coherent; that is, some of my beliefs do not contradict others.

_____ I can explain and defend my beliefs capably.

_____ I am a good listener.

_____ I am objective and even-handed in my assessments. I do not exaggerate the benefits or harms of a belief, an argument, a person, an organization, a life style, a movement, a product or a service.

_____ I know that my perceptions can be distorted by my expectations, beliefs, biases and state of mind.

_____ I know that my memory is selective and constructive, and seldom provides a literal report of past events.

_____ I appreciate the important role of skepticism in my life, refusing to embrace a claim, however satisfying or intriguing, until I find reasonable grounds for it.

_____ I am open-minded and flexible. I am willing to consider a different perspective on an issue than the one that I am used to taking, and I am willing to hear or read an elaboration and defense of a claim which strikes me initially as weird or far-fetched.

_____ I am sensitive to my own fallibility, that is, my proneness as a human being to make mistakes. I have the courage to acknowledge the possibility that a long-cherished belief on mine may be mistaken.

_____ I successfully detect bias, propaganda, special pleading, code words and exaggeration in what I hear and read.

_____ I am aware that many television programs, films and publications deviate from the historical record and contradict well-established scientific laws and theories.

_____ I strive to stay intellectually alive. I regularly read books, newspapers, magazines and other publications. I balance my reading so that I expose myself to a variety of views and perspectives. I participate regularly in serious, civil conversations about significant issues in the news.

_____ I understand and detect common fallacies in reasoning, including begging the question (assuming what one is supposed to prove); the appeal to ignorance (assuming the correctness of a claim because it has not been disproved); stereotyping and hasty generalization (jumping to a conclusion based upon one or few observations); post hoc ergo propter hoc (assuming that because one event preceded another the former cause the latter); ad hominem (disqualifying an argument because of its presenter and not its merit); the appeal to authority (sanctioning a claim based solely on its advocate or supporter); and the slippery slope (assuming that a modest change will necessarily trigger dire consequences).

_____ I strive to avoid the use of such fallacies in my own reasoning.

_____ TOTAL

The highest score possible is 90. How did you do?

Now if you are especially bold and brave, you might invite another person to evaluate your critical thinking skills on this test and then compare the two scores. Remember, good thinking, like good health, is a lifelong challenge.

Checkpoint

Critical thinker?

How did you score? Are you a critical thinker? Want to become a better critical thinker?

_____

_____

_____

What is critical thinking? Brown and Keeley (2009) define **critical thinking** as the:

1. Awareness of a set of interrelated critical questions
2. Ability to ask and answer critical questions at appropriate times
3. Desire to actively use the critical questions

But first, in order to be a critical thinker, you need to be able to flex two different kinds of thinking muscles: absorbing information like a sponge and actively panning for gold.

Sponge

Panning for Gold

Sveltlana Lukienko/Shutterstock.com

Dawn Hudson/Shutterstock.com

When you absorb information, like a sponge, you are obtaining foundational factual knowledge that will allow you to then pan for the gold, or nuggets of thought, as a critical thinker. You cannot know what you are looking for when you pan for gold if you don't have the factual knowledge to know what gold looks like. You might end up with pyrite instead (fool's gold)! Below are some of the differences between reading like a sponge or panning for gold.

Sponge	Panning for Gold
Reads carefully	Reader asks self a number of questions to uncover the best available decisions or beliefs
Remembers as much as possible	
Underlines/highlights	Questions the author's claims
Takes notes summarizing main points/topics	
Mission is to find and understand what the author says	Makes notes in the margins indicating problems with reasoning
Memorizes reasoning	
Doesn't evaluate	Forms own conclusion

To extend the metaphor a little more, we can see that being a sponge might be a bit passive whereas panning for gold is an active process that requires you to interact (shake the pan) with the information in order to assess what is true and what is questionable. So what are some questions to ask yourself while you read?

Purpose	What is the author's purpose? Is it clearly stated?
Topic	Is there a well-written question? Is the topic unbiased and linked to the purpose?
Evidence	Are there relevant sources used? Are they accurate?
Assumptions	Does the author explain or address assumptions?
Point of View	Does the author consider alternative reasoning or respond to the "cons" to their argument?
Consequences	What are the implications of the position the author is taking?

Now that you have some ideas about what kinds of questions to ask as a critical thinker, you need to ask and answer those critical questions at appropriate times — while reading, and while discussing with study partners, in-class discussions, office hours, and with tutors or others. And finally, you need to desire, or want, to ask the questions.

Checkpoint

Why is it important to read your textbooks in college? _____

_____

Why is it important to read any additional reading assignments in your courses?

_____

Why read outside of class? _____

Having a purpose for the reading you do allows you to focus on specific reading strategies to make your reading more effective. Reading "just because I have to for class" or "the professor said so" is not a sufficient purpose for reading! Having a purpose will also help to motivate you to get the reading completed. Some classes are heavily dependent on lecture notes and the books are used as supplementary material. Some reading (usually textbooks) is critical because the information might be discussed in class or not, but you are still responsible for knowing the information for an exam.

The first speed bump for most students will be managing **executive functioning**, or cognitive processes like planning and execution. **Metacognition** is defined as "knowing about knowing" and includes two components, the initial knowledge about cognition and the regulation of that cognition (Zadina, Smilkstein, Daiek, & Anter, 2014). It is not enough to merely know what good students do as they read; you have to be willing to think about your reading and task management as it happens in order to assess if you are applying those best practices. If you are not applying best practices, having the flexibility to change is also part of metacognition. Simply stated, metacognition is thinking before, during, and after a task — in this case, reading. Listed below are some areas of executive functioning, as they relate to college reading and some strategies for managing them.

Executive Functioning Area	Strategies
Forgetting reading assignments?	Develop a reminder system that works for you: to-do list, write all reading tasks on a master calendar, set appointment reminders in your phone.
Managing time ineffectively?	Try the power hours mentioned in the third chapter or try "chunking" the chapter into more manageable pieces.
Easily distracted while reading?	Metacognitively check for distractions, then plan what you do to recover from them. Take a breath, stretch, and then dive back in. If you aren't sure how often you get distracted, try keeping a little sticky note where you make a checkmark each time you get distracted.
Don't have the necessary knowledge to understand what you are reading or find it difficult?	Take time to pause while reading and make a list of questions or complicated vocabulary, or potentially even stop and read some foundational information first, in order to better understand what is presented in the text.
Find yourself on autopilot where pages have passed but you don't recall anything?	Many times this is associated with excessive highlighting or passive reading. Try some of the active reading strategies listed below.

Checkpoint

What executive functioning area do you need improvement in? _____

_____

Which strategy will you apply? _____

_____

COMPREHENSION STRATEGIES
By Kate Tiller

Ready to try to improve your comprehension of what you read? "Good readers know when they are confused and do something to get themselves unstuck" (Tovani, 2000). Try one or both of these strategies to uncover your comprehension challenges.

Sticky Notes in Sticky Places
Grab a pad of sticky notes and when you read, place a sticky note where you become confused. On that sticky note describe your confusion. Explain why you don't "get it." It might be an unfamiliar word, a reference to something you don't know, or even that your mind wandered. Now, find a friend and see if they were stuck in some of the same places. By sharing with others you will start to construct meaning and better understand the reading.

Highlighting for Comprehension
Ready to monitor your comprehension again? Get a pink and yellow highlighter. Highlight every word of a short passage, either in pink or yellow. If you understand it well enough to teach it to someone else, then highlight it pink. If you didn't understand it, then highlight it yellow. Everyone is going to understand different portions and have questions about different portions. That's reading. We don't make meaning by being passive absorbers of information. We make meaning by interacting with the text.

Scenic Overlook

Would you read all of these texts the same way?
- an introductory chemistry textbook
- an essay by prominent social theorists
- a first-hand account of a historical event
- a brief poem
- a magazine advertisement
- a novel, for pleasure
- a novel, for literary analysis
- an update on Facebook or Twitter

What are you supposed to be getting out of reading for your various classes?

To be a good reader you have to understand that there are different types of reading tasks and not all were meant for you, the student. How "considerate" is the text? That is, does the text (and the author) think about the reader when writing? Obviously, textbooks are meant for you and give you lots of resources to aide you in reading (bold-faced words, index, table of contents, glossary, diagrams, etc.) However, research articles are not written for students or laypersons. These are written for those in their academic discipline and therefore present numerous reading speed bumps such as academic jargon, research methods, and statistics. Primary sources, those original documents from the time period being studied, are another kind of reading that you might have to tackle which require their own set of finesse.

Course type	Reading Purpose	End Product
Social sciences	Learn facts and definitions	Build to concepts or generalizations (flex inductive thinking)
Humanities (art, literature, music, philosophy)	Draw logical inferences and implications	Keep track of personal reactions in marginal or separate notes
Mathematics	Translate abstract formulas into common sense language	Identify and contrast new theorems and formulas
Natural sciences (astronomy, biology, chemistry, physics, geology)	Read for common patterns	Analyze sample problems

But no matter the type of reading, you should match the reading purpose with a coordinating speed. Below is a chart that explains the four main **reading rates** and their corresponding purposes (Wong, 2015).

	Purpose	Which class would you use this reading rate for?
Recreational reading	For pleasure	
Overview reading	To ask questions; prep for class; gain a general understanding; to participate in class discussion	
Thorough reading	To be quizzed on key vocabulary or tested generally	
Comparative reading	To lead a discussion or write a paper	

"Don't just read the easy stuff. You may be entertained by it, but you will never grow from it." ~ Jim Rohn

If you know you have a straightaway and are not turning any time soon, you can increase your speed and set your cruise control. It is important that if you pass a signpost or warning sign (bold-faced words, call-out boxes, charts, diagrams, reflective questions, check-ins), that you slow down and pay attention. Have you played with your reading rate? What does it feel like to skim versus read thoroughly? It is important to flex your reading speed to meet your reading purpose and know that it is okay to skim. Allow yourself to skim. It is better than not reading at all, right?

Additionally, some students have a negative association with reading because of labels put on them, such as being a "slow reader," but there are many strategies that can be employed to make reading a more pleasurable activity.

- Read something you enjoy for 15 to 20 minutes without stopping.
- Set reading-rate goals for yourself. Aim for a 10% increase in your reading rate over the previous record.
- Record your reading rate and chart your progress as you schedule time to read in your calendar.
- Push yourself gently as you read. If your mind wanders, get it back on track.
- Practice skimming and scanning by finding an interesting newspaper column or magazine article and rapidly reading the article, sampling just the first sentence or two of each paragraph and a few key words. Jot down all the facts you can remember. Then reread the article slowly, giving yourself a point for every item you recalled. How did you do?
- Make a word list of challenging vocabulary that you can look up later online (most online dictionaries even have an audio button where you can hear someone read the word aloud).
- Find a list of root words (Internet or on a phone app) and play with them (kind of like puzzle pieces) in order to see how they are the building blocks of all language.

ONLINE READING & TECHNOLOGY TOOLS

Reading online articles or e-textbooks presents a different challenge to students. Online reading can lead to lower levels of interactivity with the text. A quick strategy would be to read a small segment at a time (paragraph or page) and then record major thoughts in a notebook. The particular speed bumps presented with online reading include eye strain (take breaks), losing a sense of location (consider printing the material), or getting lost in a string of details (take good notes to place yourself in the reading). Some other speed bumps already discussed are distractions (shut down your applications like email, Netflix, and Facebook) and auto pilot (pause and take good notes at small vantage points).

When doing online research (in electronic databases, for instance):

- Skim through the article to see if it contains relevant material.
- Save the article to your computer so you can sit down with all downloaded articles at some later point and assess if they really meet your research goals.
- Once you have picked your set of articles, annotate them electronically or you can print them out but always keep your purpose in mind.

Consider these technology tools (if available) to assist you with reading:

- KIC Scanner: this scanner can turn text into audio recording or create a searchable PDF from your paper texts.
- Pocket, Readability, Instapaper, etc.
- Change to dark background and light words, select the biggest font possible.
- Calibrate your screen for reading (turn on portrait mode).

Can you see reading as a journey? There are lots of reading "methods" and what is laid out below will give you a step-by-step method. Good readers are adaptable and might use a few or all strategies depending on their reading purpose. Remember that metacognition is thinking before, during, and after reading — constantly monitoring your brain activity.

CREATING AN IDEAL READING ENVIRONMENT _ _ _ _ _ _

Follow these steps to create the best environment for reading:

o Plan time on your daily schedule for reading and leave adequate buffer time to complete reading assignments, until you know exactly how long it will take you to read a certain amount of pages.

o Do not schedule reading time for a time in the day when you are tired (or in bed). If you find yourself falling asleep, take a nap! Do not keep reading as that would be a waste of time since you aren't using active reading strategies at this point. Just take a break and come back refreshed and ready to read actively.

o Try not to read in your room. There are a lot of distractions, plus a bed to sleep in. Pick a location that either matches your purpose (for inspiration), or a place that matches your comfort level without visual and auditory distractions. If you need complete quiet to read and retain, read in that environment. On the other hand, if you find you need some level of visual/auditory distraction to keep you focused and awake, read in that environment.

BEFORE READING

1. Set your purpose.
2. Assess your level of background or prior knowledge.
3. Create questions that you can and should be able to answer when you are finished reading.
4. Set your time.

ACTIVE READING STRATEGIES

The first step in **active reading** is to take reading notes of some sort. In order to be an active reader, you need to do certain things to keep your brain involved in the reading process. You need to be thinking while you read instead of passively taking in information. Don't forget to be:

o Monitoring comprehension
o Making associations
o Challenging or adjusting existing schemata (or your knowledge base)
o Deciding what needs to be remembered and how it will be committed to memory
o Determining what needs to be checked, what sources to consult, and what can be skipped

How can you process it all while you read? There are many options:

1. **Annotate** in the margins. These are opportunities to note important key ideas (draw a key), make lists, write vocabulary definitions in your own words, etc.

2. **Take notes** in a notebook (preferably one that has your class notes in it too) so that you can start to compare class notes and text notes and integrate them into one another. This format allows you to take notes in a more linear or outline format. Consider writing notes from class on the front of pages and reading notes that connect to the class notes on the back of pages.

3. **Paraphrase** what you read into your own words and consider using small sticky notes on each paragraph, page, or section in order to force that summarization.
4. Consider **alternative note taking** formats such as:
    *   Creating a concept map to show the relationship among aspects of a concept or principle
    *   Creating a flow chart or timeline
    *   Creating PowerPoint slides, like you are preparing to teach the information to someone
    *   Constructing tables or graphs
    *   Learning vocabulary by creating notecards for each term
5. **Interact with the text** in advanced ways such as:
    *   Creating questions while you read
    *   Generating examples or making connections
    *   Making predictions about where the text is headed
    *   Predicting test questions
6. The last resort is to underline or highlight your text. Most people recommend reading a page and then going back to highlight text that is important to revisit later. Only about 10% or less of the text on a page should be highlighted or underlined.

MARK UP YOUR TEXTBOOK

By Nathalie Rhodes-Vega
Associate Mathematics Professor, Lone Star College-Kingwood

As a math professor, I've noticed a trend when people read math textbooks: usually, the only pages that are used are the ones containing exercise sets. While these pages are important, many hidden gems exist on the pages between these exercise sets! Let's take a look at how a good reader would annotate their math textbook:

3.1 Introduction to Signed Fractions

☐ Prepare   **☐ Organize**

What are your objectives for Section 3.1?	How can you accomplish each objective?
1 Understand What Fractions Represent	• Write your own definition of a *fraction*, and include the words *numerator* and *denominator*. • Complete the given examples on your own. • Complete You Trys 1 and 2.
2 Identify Proper and Improper Fractions	• Write the definition of a *proper fraction* and *improper fraction* in your own words, and be sure to include the words *numerator* and *denominator*. • Compare the relationship between the numerator and the denominator in the definitions. • Complete the given examples on your own. • Complete You Trys 3-4.
3 Understand Negative Fractions	• Explain, in your own words, the meaning of the absolute value of a fraction. • Explain how to graph a negative fraction on a number line. • Complete the given example on your own. • Complete You Try 5.

W Work   Read the explanations, follow the examples, take notes, and complete the You Trys.

Until now, we have been working with integers, sometimes known as the positive and negative counting numbers. We can list the integers like this:

$$\ldots, -5, -4, -3, -2, -1, 0, 1, 2, 3, 4, 5, \ldots$$

But what if we need a number to represent a *part* of a whole? We can use fractions.

1 Understand What Fractions Represent

What is a *fraction*? A **fraction** is a part of a whole. We will look at some figures and number lines to understand fractions. Let's begin with a circle divided into three equal parts.

Each of these parts is *one-third*, or $\frac{1}{3}$, of the circle.

The number $\frac{1}{3}$ is an example of a fraction.

If I eat one piece of pizza with 8 slices, I ate $\frac{1}{8}$ of the pizza.

158   CHAPTER 3   Operations with Signed Fractions   www.mhhe.com/messersmith

From *Pre-algebra with P.O.W.E.R. Learning* by Sherri Messersmith, et al.
Copyright © 2014 by McGraw-Hill Education. Reprinted by permission.

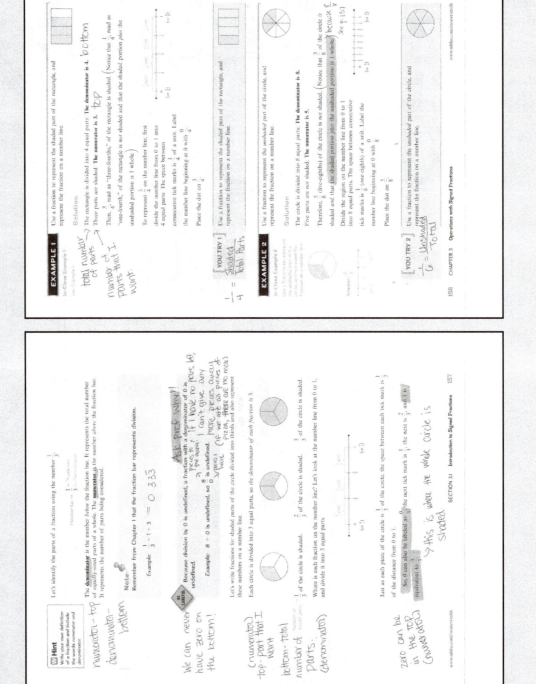

Hint
Write your own definition of a fraction and include the words numerator and denominator

Let's identify the parts of a fraction using the number $\frac{1}{3}$.

$$\text{Fraction bar} \rightarrow \frac{1}{3} \leftarrow \text{Numerator} \atop \leftarrow \text{Denominator}$$

The **denominator** is the number *below* the fraction bar. It represents the total number of equally-sized parts of a whole. The **numerator** is the number *above* the fraction bar. It represents the number of parts being considered.

Note
Remember from Chapter 1 that the fraction bar represents division.

Example: $\frac{1}{3} = 1 \div 3 = 0.333$

BE CAREFUL
Because division by 0 is undefined, a fraction with a denominator of 0 is undefined.

Example: $8 \div 0$ is undefined, so $\frac{8}{0}$ is undefined.

Let's write fractions for shaded parts of the circle divided into 3 equal parts, so *the denominator of each fraction is 3*.

Each circle is divided into 3 equal parts, so the denominator of each fraction is 3.

$\frac{1}{3}$ of the circle is shaded. $\frac{2}{3}$ of the circle is shaded. $\frac{3}{3}$ of the circle is shaded.

Just as each fraction on the number line? Let's look at the number line from 0 to 1, and divide it into 3 equal parts.

Where is each fraction on the number line...

Just as each piece of the circle is $\frac{1}{3}$ of the circle, the space between each tick mark is $\frac{1}{3}$ of the distance from 0 to 1.

So 0 can also be labeled as $\frac{0}{3}$; the next tick mark is $\frac{1}{3}$; the next is $\frac{2}{3}$; and 1 is equivalent to $\frac{3}{3}$.

Handwritten notes:
numerator- top of parts that I want
denominator- bottom

We can never have zero on the bottom!

(numerator) top- part that I want
bottom- total number of parts (denominator)

zero can be the top in (numerator)

ASK PROF WHY! If I have no pieces left to give away, I can't give any more pieces away. (if we eat all pieces of pizza, there are no more)

→ this is where the whole circle is shaded

EXAMPLE 1

Use a fraction to represent the shaded part of the rectangle, and represent the fraction on a number line.

Solution

The rectangle is divided into 4 equal parts. **The denominator is 4.**

Three parts are shaded. **The numerator is 3.**

Then, $\frac{3}{4}$, read as "three-fourths," of the rectangle is shaded and that the shaded portion *plus* the unshaded portion is 1 whole.

To represent $\frac{3}{4}$ on the number line, first divide the number line from 0 to 1 into 4 equal parts. The space between consecutive tick marks is $\frac{1}{4}$ of a unit. Label the number line beginning at 0 with $\frac{0}{4}$.

Place the dot on $\frac{3}{4}$.

YOU TRY 1

Handwritten:
total number of parts → bottom
number of parts that I want → top
$\frac{3}{4} = \dfrac{\text{Shaded}}{\text{Total Parts}}$

EXAMPLE 2

Use a fraction to represent the *unshaded* part of the circle, and represent the fraction on a number line.

Solution

The circle is divided into 8 equal parts. **The denominator is 8.**

Five parts are *not* shaded. **The numerator is 5.**

Therefore, $\frac{5}{8}$ (five-eighths) of the circle is *not* shaded. (Notice that $\frac{3}{8}$ of the circle *is* shaded and that the unshaded portion *plus* the shaded portion is 1 whole.) because $\frac{5}{8} + \frac{3}{8} = \frac{8}{8}$ See p.151

Divide the region on the number line from 0 to 1 into 8 equal parts. The space between consecutive tick marks is $\frac{1}{8}$ (one-eighth) of a unit. Label the number line beginning at 0 with $\frac{0}{8}$.

Place the dot on $\frac{5}{8}$.

YOU TRY 2

Handwritten:
$\dfrac{5}{6} = \dfrac{\text{Unshaded}}{\text{Total}}$

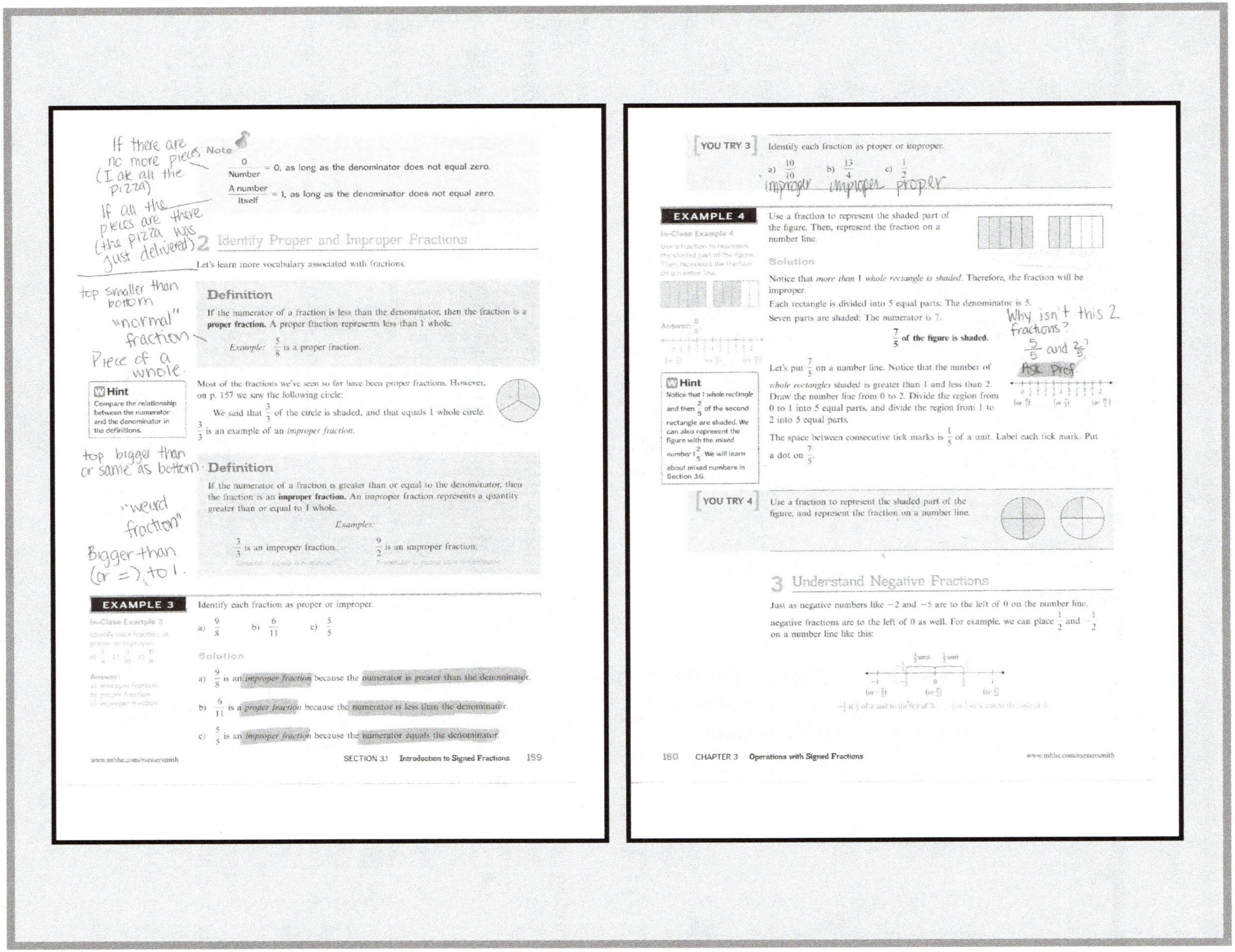

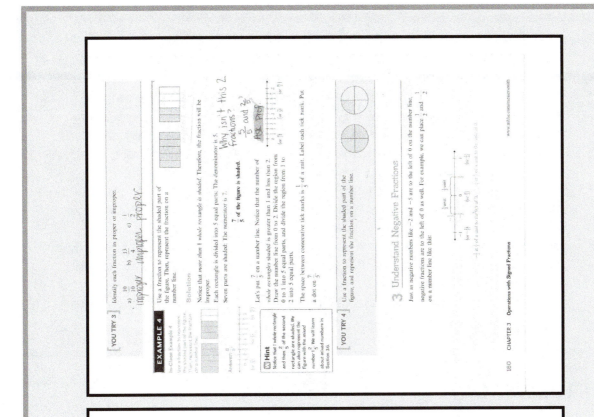

Handwritten note: *If there are no more pieces (I took all the pizza) was just divided.*

Note:

$$\frac{0}{\text{Number}} = 0, \text{ as long as the denominator does not equal zero.}$$

$$\frac{\text{A number}}{\text{itself}} = 1, \text{ as long as the denominator does not equal zero.}$$

Handwritten: top smaller than bottom "normal" fraction. Piece of a whole.

Let's learn more vocabulary associated with fractions.

Identify Proper and Improper Fractions

Definition

If the numerator of a fraction is less than the denominator, then the fraction is a **proper fraction.** A proper fraction represents less than 1 whole.

Example: $\frac{5}{8}$ is a *proper fraction.*

Most of the fractions we've seen so far have been proper fractions. However, on p. 157 we saw the following circle:

We said that $\frac{3}{3}$ of the circle is shaded, and that equals 1 whole circle.

$\frac{3}{3}$ is an example of an *improper fraction.*

Definition

If the numerator of a fraction is greater than or equal to the denominator, then the fraction is an **improper fraction.** An improper fraction represents a quantity greater than or equal to 1 whole.

Handwritten: top bigger than or same as bottom. "weird fraction" Bigger than (or =) to 1.

Example:

$\frac{3}{3}$ is an improper fraction.

$\frac{9}{3}$ is an improper fraction.

Hint
Compare the relationship between the numerator and the denominator in the definitions.

EXAMPLE 3

Identify each fraction as proper or improper.

a) $\frac{9}{8}$ b) $\frac{6}{11}$ c) $\frac{5}{5}$

Solution

a) $\frac{9}{8}$ is an *improper fraction* because the numerator is greater than the denominator.

b) $\frac{6}{11}$ is a *proper fraction* because the numerator is less than the denominator.

c) $\frac{5}{5}$ is an *improper fraction* because the numerator equals the denominator.

SECTION 3.1   Introduction to Signed Fractions   159

[YOU TRY 3]

Identify each fraction as proper or improper.

a) $\frac{10}{10}$ b) $\frac{13}{4}$ c) $\frac{1}{2}$

Handwritten: improper, improper, proper

EXAMPLE 4

Use a fraction to represent the shaded part of the figure. Then, represent the fraction on a number line.

Solution

Notice that *more than 1 whole rectangle is shaded.* Therefore, the fraction will be improper.

Each rectangle is divided into 5 equal parts. The denominator is 5.

Seven parts are shaded: The numerator is 7.

$\frac{7}{5}$ **of the figure is shaded.**

Let's put $\frac{7}{5}$ on a number line. Notice that the number of *whole rectangles shaded* is greater than 1 and less than 2. Draw the number line from 0 to 2. Divide the region from 0 to 1 into 5 equal parts, and divide the region from 1 to 2 into 5 equal parts.

The space between consecutive tick marks is $\frac{1}{5}$ of a unit. Label each tick mark. Put a dot on $\frac{7}{5}$.

Handwritten: Why isn't this 2 fractions? $\frac{5}{5}$ and $\frac{2}{5}$ ASK PROF

Hint
Notice that 1 whole rectangle and then $\frac{2}{5}$ of the second rectangle are shaded. We can also represent the figure with the mixed number $1\frac{2}{5}$. We will learn about mixed numbers in Section 3.6.

[YOU TRY 4]

Use a fraction to represent the shaded part of the figure, and represent the fraction on a number line.

3 Understand Negative Fractions

Just as negative numbers like -2 and -5 are to the left of 0 on the number line, negative fractions are to the right of 0 as well. For example, we can place $\frac{1}{2}$ and $-\frac{1}{2}$ on a number line like this:

160   CHAPTER 3   Operations with Signed Fractions

The tips below will show you how to get the most out of your math textbook to help you be successful in your math classes.

- Look at the goals and objectives at the start of each section *before* your instructor covers that section in class. This will give you a good understanding of what you will be expected to learn in that section.
- Note any words with special formatting (large print, **bold** print, *italics*, etc.). Take special note of these words; you should know what each one means. Since mathematics is a subject that builds on itself, you will want to have a general understanding of these words by the end of the section. You may consider creating flash cards with these words.
- Take special note of any colored boxes. These boxes typically contain useful information - definitions, formulas, procedures, important information, or common mistakes that students make. These also make good flash cards.
- Your text has wide margins with blank space for you to use! As you are reading, jot down any questions you have about the material. You can ask these questions in class or during office hours. Write down any notes from these discussions to help later during review.
- You can also use the blank space of the margins to work examples in the text. As you work, compare your method to that of the text. If you find any differences, you can ask this question in class. Highlight these discrepancies so you can remember the issues when you are reviewing.
- Take a last look at the goals and objectives listed at the start of the section. Now that you've read the applicable material, do you understand what each one means?

AFTER READING

Now that you are finished reading, you are not done yet! Here are some items to do after you are finished reading a chapter or portion:

1. Summarize what you read. Choose the most important pieces to write down. These can trigger your memory later.
2. Check the questions you created (or the ones your textbook presents) to see if you have an answer to them.
3. Review your notes to make sure they make sense.
4. Consider trying to teach what you know to someone else to reinforce your reading or form a study group session to discuss the readings.
5. Go to class and check your knowledge — ask clarifying questions.
6. Consider rereading a portion after class to clarify what was discussed in class. It might help you hone in on the most important parts.

You are being asked to balance lots of tasks on daily basis and it is important that creating a weekly reading plan is part of that. This requires that you can accurately estimate how long it takes to read certain materials and then lay out times in your schedule to get these things done. You can test this with your class materials by using a textbook chapter as your test chapter and notate how long it takes to read it.

Checkpoint

Use this grid to show how you would schedule enough time to read your texts before you went to class. Make sure to give each reading a specific block of time and enough time.

	Mon.	Tues.	Wed.	Thurs.	Fri.	Sat.	Sun.
7 am							
8 am							
9 am							
10 am							
11 am							
Noon							
1 pm							
2 pm							
3 pm							
4 pm							
5 pm							
6 pm							
7 pm							
8 pm							
9 pm							
10 pm							
11 pm							
Midnight							

SUMMARY

Hopefully you have learned more about what good readers do and that you must set a purpose for reading and monitor your comprehension as you read. There are several factors that affect the reading of text that you must keep in mind as you tackle more and more challenging texts:

Reader factors:

- o Understanding task demands (Do you understand the reading that you have been assigned and how it fits into the overall course?)
- o Background content knowledge (What do you previously know about this? Do you need to do some background reading first, before you tackle this particular reading?)
- o Motivation (Are you motivated to read this passage?)
- o Reading ability (Do you have the ability to read this passage or is it too advanced? Do you have a reading disability that might stand in the way of accomplishing this reading?)

Text factors:

- o **Considerateness** of the text (Does the author consider you while writing?)
- o Readability (Is the vocabulary and syntax on a level that the reader can grasp?)
- o Features (Do the font, graphics, use of bold type, white space, and color make the text accessible?)

Situational factors:

- o Assignment due date (If it is a pressing deadline, you might feel more stressed and less able to focus.)
- o Concurrent commitments (Are you reading but thinking about other issues in your life?)
- o Physical factors such as sleep needs, emotional state, and resources available (Are you in a good physical condition in order to give your readings your full attention?)

Good readers consider all of these factors and utilize active reading strategies in order to absorb text information, then critically question that information. Thinking about your readings before, during, and after you have accomplished them will improve your metacognitive ability and hopefully, in turn, improve your academic ability.

Scenic Overlook————————————

How has your understanding of reading as a process changed from before? What active reading strategy will you try as a result of reading this chapter?

_____

_____

Rev Your Engine

1. Want to tackle some of these logical fallacies that were discussed at the beginning of the chapter? Find a pop culture or recent news reference for each one:

Logical Fallacy	Definition	Pop Culture Reference
Ad hominem	Disqualifying an argument because of its presenter and not its merit	President Bush called the Argentinian President the "devil" and refused to work with him
Begging the question	Assuming what one is supposed to prove	
Equivocation	Using the same word in different senses	
Appeal to ignorance	Assuming the correctness of a claim because it has not been disproved	
Stereotyping	Jumping to a conclusion based upon one or few observations	
Post hoc ergo propter hoc	Assuming that because one event preceded another, the former caused the latter	
Appeal to authority	Sanctioning a claim based solely on its advocate or supporters	
Slippery slope	Assuming that a modest change will necessarily trigger dire consequences	

2. Take some controversial issue that you have a deep-set belief about (such as abortion, gun control, the death penalty) and argue the other side. You know your side well but to be a critical thinker requires that you understand the con to your argument at all times. Why would someone argue something different than you? Are you an agile enough thinker to argue the other side?

REFERENCES

Brown, M.N., & Keeley S.M. (2009). *Asking the Right Questions: A Guide to Critical Thinking.* Upper Saddle River, NJ: Pearson Prentice Hall.

McGrath, J.L. (2005). *Strategies for Critical Reading.* Upper Saddle River, NJ: Pearson Prentice Hall.

Tovani, C. (2009). *I read it, but I don't get it: Comprehension Strategies for Adolescent Readers.* Portland, ME: Stenhouse Publishers.

Wong, L. (2015). *Essential Study Skills.* Stamford, CT: Cengage Learning.

Zadina, J.N., Smilkstein, R., Daiek, D.B., & Anter, N.M. (2014). *College Reading: The Science and Strategies of Expert Readers.* Stamford, CT: Cengage Learning.

POST TEST/QUIZ

1. Two approaches to thinking are being a _____ and _____ _____ _____.

2. It is better to read faster for more important reading material. T F

3. Define metacognition. How should metacognitive study strategies impact your studying?

4. What are three metacognitive reading strategies that you can use—one before, one during, and one after reading?

CHAPTER 5

STUDYING AND NOTE TAKING: THE ROAD SCHOLAR

By Melissa Hortman

1. **LEARNING OUTCOMES: QUESTIONS TO NAVIGATE**
    a. Why is studying important to being successful in college?
    b. What are the steps to studying material before a test?
    c. Why is note taking important to learning material?
    d. What does effective listening look like?
    e. What is the most effective way to study material?
    f. What are some common barriers while studying?
    g. What is the importance of knowing your learning modality?

2. **KEY CONCEPTS**
    a. Building healthy study habits
    b. Study pyramid
    c. Handwriting notes
    d. Note taking cycle
    e. Listening
    f. Reviewing notes
    g. Study methods
    h. Study barriers
    i. Learning modalities
    j. Multiple Intelligences

INTRODUCTION

What sounds more enjoyable, "studying" or "learning"? Learning has a more positive connotation when it comes to sitting and looking over material for a test. Change your thinking about studying to "learning" and it becomes a much more enjoyable experience!

Studying is not something that happens the day before an exam. You can **build healthy study habits** by integrating the pre, during, and post test-taking process into your lifestyle to make it just part of your everyday life. Studying is the driving within your journey; it needs to be done every day to get to your destination of success. Studying is not just sitting over a book and reading information, re-reading it, and re-re-reading it. It's the action of learning each and every day to keep the material fresh in your mind as you acquire new knowledge. To truly learn is to recall previous knowledge and tie it back to newly learned information. Have you ever tried to learn a new skill you knew nothing about? It is very difficult to learn a new skill without having some experience or foundational knowledge of how to do it. It actually takes 10,000 hours to master a new skill, which is why you are required to take so many college courses in an area — to master it. (But don't lose hope — it only takes 40 hours of active practice in order to become reasonably good at something.)

Do you ever find that some skills come easier to you than others? The way your brain works and the way you learn, as well as what you are drawn to affects how you approach studying. By knowing this, you can be more efficient in the time you spend studying. You cannot instantly reach your destination — you need to know what the necessary steps are to get there successfully!

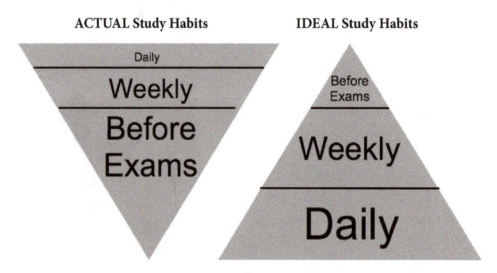

As you see in the Actual vs. Ideal Studying Habits diagram above, the triangle on the left shows the studying habits of many students. Most of studying is done right before the exam; not a lot of the studying is done on a daily or weekly basis other than going to class and taking notes. With the left triangle, most of the time spent studying for an exam is trying to learn all the information crammed into a short time period right before the exam. When you cram, the information goes in as fast as it leaves because it is only stored in short-term memory. You do not want to put all of this effort into studying for a test just to forget the information.

Now look at the triangle on the right side. Only a small amount of time is spent on studying right before an exam. When more effort is put into studying on a daily and weekly basis, you become more efficient in the way you are learning material and a minimal amount of study time is needed before the exam. Think of this time as just a review for the exam. When studying is done on a daily and weekly basis, you are moving the previous knowledge to long-term memory while keeping up with learning new information along the way. So flip your thinking about studying and flip your triangle to put a little bit more effort on the front end to be more successful in the end! Don't know what to do on a weekly basis? Keep reading for tips on active study strategies!

In this chapter, you will learn about the middle levels of the study pyramid: attending (listening and note taking) and reviewing (drawing connections after class). We will look at the study cycle, note taking and memory, study strategies, and learning modalities. Each of these topics falls under attending and reviewing, which is a critical piece to learning material in a more effective and efficient way.

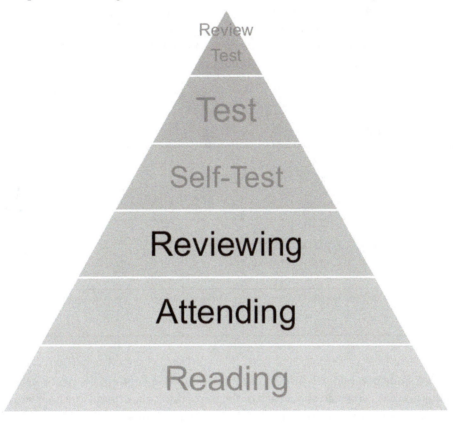

STUDY PYRAMID

Studying is more than sitting down the night before an exam and looking over all the notes you have taken since the last test. It is a progression that begins on the first day of class and continues even after a test is taken. Each step in the progression needs to be recognized and fulfilled before moving on to the next. Think about it as a sequence that can be applied from the first day of class to the first test, restarting the sequence after each test. When applied correctly, this pyramid can help you truly learn information by maximizing your productivity at all times throughout the learning process.

There are many benefits to thinking about studying through this **study pyramid**. The first and foremost is that it eliminates the need for cramming. Cramming does not allow the brain time to process the information and store it; you are not gaining any previous knowledge to tie material back to because you are learning it all at once. With the sequence of the study pyramid, you must go through each of the steps, allotting time for each step and between each step, thus eliminating the need for cramming. Another benefit of the study pyramid is that it promotes shorter, more active study sessions. You cannot complete all of the steps to the pyramid in one sitting; they must be broken up into different study sessions. Thus, the shorter sessions help you be more efficient because you are not over-extending what your brain can do. The average person can sit and focus their attention for around 30-40 minutes at a time. That is the total amount of time you should be studying in one sitting before taking a break. The next time you sit down to study, when you start drifting off, checking emails, or getting distracted, check your watch, it will probably be at the 30-40 minute mark. Break up your studying into the steps within the pyramid and you will naturally create these shorter study sessions that are better for your brain. The most helpful benefit to using this study pyramid is that it can help you retain information for longer periods of time. Think about learning something and remembering it weeks later for an exam, even further away for a final exam in the course, and furthest to use as previous knowledge for the next course in that sequence.

Checkpoint

What are some other words that could replace "attending" in this study pyramid?

_____

What are some other words that could replace "reviewing" in this study pyramid?

_____

_____

Each step in the study pyramid will be discussed much more in depth in the next sections as well as the next chapter in this book. As you read about each of the steps, think about ways in which you can apply them to your current courses and how that looks in your time management schedule.

NOTE TAKING AND MEMORY

"Note taking is seen as the rapid transcription of information by using a few condensing techniques, such as shortened words and substitutions symbols, for the creation of an external memory whose only importance will be its later use."
~ Boch and Piolat (2005)

Taking notes is a very important piece to the journey and falls under the "attending" step in the study pyramid. Taking notes in class can help you learn information better so that you can remember it at a later time. You are creating an external memory so that you can review the notes after class to draw connections.

HANDWRITTEN NOTES

Current research has shown that there are many benefits to taking **handwritten notes** in class, which ultimately helps you remember information. Below are some of those benefits:

- When you handwrite, you are stimulating the brain's highest cognition because of muscle memory. Do you ever feel like you can remember information you write down or write down multiple times? You have experienced muscle memory at work!

- As you take notes in class, be sure to be selective in what you write down. Do not try to write down every word. The average lecturer speaks approximately 125-140 words per minute, and the average note-taker writes at a rate of about 25 words per minute. You should not aspire to be a court stenographer. Instead, give your brain time to reflect as you write. The slower speed of writing forces you to decide what is the most important point to include in your notes.

- When you take notes you enhance your brain's intake, processing, retaining, and retrieving of the information heard and learned. There is more focus and attention to what you write because information has to go through various steps in your mind before and as you are writing, such as assessing, sorting, and coding.

- Taking notes can help prevent you from being distracted when you are sitting in class.

- Taking notes in class is simply better for learning. The act of taking notes facilitates both recall of factual information and the synthesis and application of new knowledge. A quick tip for taking notes: translate ideas into your own words. This will help you synthesize information, understand it, and put it in words you will remember at a later time.

- If nothing else, taking notes will make you a better writer. You begin to understand the pieces of the whole and develop a complex way of deciding what to record.

Checkpoint

Why is handwriting your notes important?_____

_____

What are some ways you can leverage handwriting to remember more in what you do now for taking notes and studying?

_____

THE NOTE-TAKING CYCLE_ _ _ _ _

As you prepare to take notes within your courses, know that it is not just a one-time occurrence. There is a cycle to note taking that can make this skill not just something you do in class because that is what everyone does, but a part of how you study and truly learn material for your courses. There are three steps within the **note-taking cycle**: the first is to observe as you prepare for class, the second is to record within class, and the third is to review by interacting with the notes after class. As you read the steps in the cycle, think how you might implement each step within your different courses while fitting each step within your days.

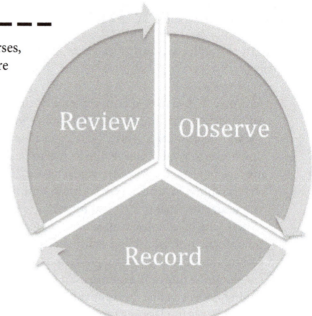

OBSERVE (To prepare for class)

Let's first look at some organizational tips when it comes to taking good notes that will help your memory. Below are some tips on how to effectively organize notes for each of your classes:

- ○ Have separate binders for each of your classes with loose-leaf paper for your notes.
- ○ Use the front side of the sheet for lecture notes and the back for corresponding notes from your readings.
- ○ Find a way to show important points in your notes.
- ○ Take notes in a format that supports your learning style.
- ○ Take notes in a format that works for the course (i.e., outline, concept map, timeline).
- ○ Leave space in your notes to fill in/annotate on at a later time.
- ○ Every class should have a different method of taking notes (but they should all be a pre, during, and post experience).
- ○ Combine these notes with those that you took from your reading and those that your professor makes available.
- ○ Recording lectures or taking a photo of the board/screen can supplement your notes.
- ○ Add some of your own organizational techniques:_____
- ○ _____
_____

RECORD (During class)

During class is the time when most students take the largest portion of their notes. The professor lectures on important information in class, connects readings, and leads discussions on topics. Below are some quick tips on how to be efficient in your note taking methods for in-class notes:

- ○ Don't bury your head in your notes; watch for non-verbal cues like a professor gesturing to a point shown.

- o You can think four times faster than your professor can talk, so use that extra time to think of examples, connect new information to last class' lecture, or evaluate what you have learned.
- o If you can't ask questions during lecture, write them in your notes to ask after class.
- o Leave space between ideas and missed points.
- o Concentrate on major ideas and write in your own words.

Three examples of types of note-taking methods in the classroom:

The Outline Method

When to use it	How to do it
• When professor has a well-organized lecture style. • When information is sequential.	• Review last class' lecture/review text reading to think of possible outline. • Be on time (or early!) for class in case professor introduces topic for day. • Listen for main ideas, subheadings, supporting points, and examples. • Organize above into informal outline – don't write too much: keep outline format.

The Graphic Organizer Method

When to use it	How to do it (one way)
• When you are a visual learner. • When you need to see connections among components.	• Identify the main ideas and supporting points. • Create a diagram/flow chart/picture that incorporates info and possible connections. • See Mind Map below for an example.

Mind Map

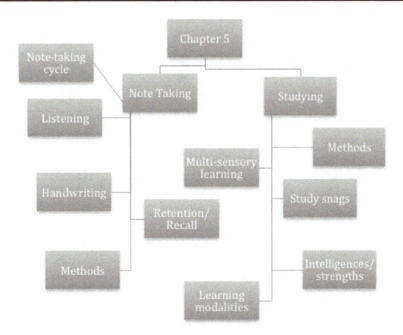

Cornell Note-Taking

When to use it	How to do it

• To keep yourself organized with a method to help you get into the structure before, during, and after class interaction with your notes.
• It can challenge your thinking about topics.
	• Use loose-leaf paper.
	• Divide each page as shown below.
	• Take notes in your preferred note taking style in the Class Notes area.
	• As soon as possible after class:
	  – Briefly summarize in your own words what was covered in lecture in the Summary of Class Notes area.
	  – Write key words, dates, formulas, questions, and other important information in the Recall Column.

<table>
<tr><td colspan="2" align="center">Date, lecture topic,

Page number, etc.</td></tr>
<tr><td>Recall Column</td><td>Class Notes</td></tr>
<tr><td colspan="2" align="center">Summary of

Class Notes</td></tr>
</table>

Not to scale

Utilize the outline method, mind map method, and Cornell note taking sheet in three separate courses, as appropriate.

CORNELL SYSTEM

Recall Column:	Class Notes:

Summary of Class Notes:

Date _____ Class _____

CORNELL SYSTEM

Recall Column:	Class Notes:

Summary of Class Notes:

Scenic Overlook _____

Look back on using the three different methods. Which method did you prefer? Did using the different methods help you listen differently in class? Was it difficult to use a different note-taking method you aren't familiar with in your courses?

As you decide what note taking method to use, think about using a different method that works effectively for you within each course to be able to utilize your notes to the fullest at pre, during, and post note taking times.

LISTENING

Being aware and **listening** in class, after having done your pre-reading for your class, can help you take effective notes. There are three levels of listening that require a certain level of concentration and sensitivity as they progress. However, as you move up the levels of listening, you also have a greater potential for understanding, retention, and effective communication.

Level One: Basic Listening
- o   Aware of the presence of others but mainly paying attention to yourself.
- o   Paying attention enough to respond once.
- o   Hearing information, but not listening to it.

Level Two: Surface Listening
- o   Listens passively, with no effort to understand.
- o   Does not have a plan for organizing thoughts.
- o   Puts information down exactly as your hear it.

Level Three: Critical Active Listening
- o   Makes connections between new information and previously learned information.
- o   Uses information in new situations.
- o   Evaluates information with regard to accuracy and relevance.

CUE WORDS

As you listen in class, be aware of cue words and phrases that speakers use to let listeners know that an important point is coming up.
- o   Words of order: first, second, next

Receiving

↓

Attending

↓

Understanding

↓

Responding

↓

Remembering

- Words indicating importance: dis/advantages of, benefits of, causes of, problems of, results of, effects of, summary of, criticism of
- Words of description: types of, kinds of, characteristics of, differences between, contrast between
- Words of function: uses, purposes, functions, steps, methods, how to, ways of
- Transition words: now, next, because, however, therefore, in addition to, in summary

Checkpoint

Communication is 40% listening, so it is an important skill to learn and practice. You listen in different ways at different times. You listen better in some situations than in others. How do your current listening skills affect your classroom experience?

_____

How do the different levels of listening affect your concentration and memory?

_____

Do you feel like you are generally a good listener?

_____

Is this different from being a good listener in class?

_____

Why or why not?

_____

REVIEW (INTERACT AFTER)

Now that you have chosen a method for note taking and actually have taken notes in class, there is one step left to complete the cycle in the note-taking process. Interacting with your notes after class by **reviewing your notes** is one of the most important steps to ensuring comprehension and remembering. However, comprehending and remembering are two separate tasks so each of these will take time, especially if you are learning new information. Material that you understand will be much easier to memorize than material that you do not understand, so be sure you complete the readings and attend class to get a foundational knowledge of the material. Below are some quick tips on what to do with your notes after class and how to interact with the material to learn it more efficiently.

After lecture	Material forgotten
20 minutes	47%
1 day	62%
2 days	69%
10 weeks	75%
15 weeks	95%
Thalheimer, W. (2010) *How much do people forget?*	

- o   Review notes and fill in gaps as soon as possible after class
- o   Review notes within several hours of class: with no review, you lose more than 50% of newly learned information (Thalheimer, 2010)
- o   Summarize the class briefly in your own words
- o   Highlight/write down words/phrases for recall column if you are using the Cornell system
- o   Combine lecture/reading notes into a condensed study guide
- o   Create study materials from notes

There are multiple ways in which you can interact with your notes during the review part of the cycle to understand and remember information. It is important to remember that comprehension and remembering are two different tasks, so the likelihood of you simply remembering information from just taking notes cannot happen. You can take notes to comprehend them, then interact with them in a focused, deep way to remember the information. Below you will find ways that you can interact with notes on different levels. Make sure to push your skills to be at the best level of interaction to remember the most from your notes!

Level of interaction	The Main Idea	How to do it
Good	Create new connections	Read over notes
Better	Focused, active reading	Highlight notes, try to only highlight up to 10 phrases
Best	Summarize notes	Re-write them in your own words, different from how you wrote them the first time (potentially typing them up, creating flashcards, or in some other form)

"We remember what we understand; we understand only what we pay attention to; we pay attention to what we want." ~ Edward Bolles

STUDY STRATEGIES_____

How did you study up to this point? What are some strengths that you have when it comes to studying? What are some challenges you have when it comes to studying? These are important questions to ask yourself as we drive into the study strategies section of this chapter. You don't know where to go unless you know where you have been.

There are many study strategies out there — this is because everyone studies differently and there are different strategies for every subject. With all of the study strategies, this is the time to try something different than you have before because the way you are studying may be ineffective for your particular learning style, course, and/or professor. Experiment with the many study strategies available for your particular situation and find what works for you; this may be a combination of one or more of the **study methods** available. Take a look at some study methods listed below:

STUDY METHODS_____

o   Rewrite notes into study sheets
o   Develop concept maps
o   Make flash cards
o   Make self-tests
o   Complete study guides
o   Re-mark text material
o   Make a list of potential topics for the exam
o   Do practice problems
o   Retake past quizzes and homework
o   Gather previous exams
o   Highlight your notes and text
o   Annotate on text and notes
o   Discuss a topic with a group
o   Utilize tutoring
o   Outline chapters and notes
o   Summarize material
o   Chart related material
o   List steps in processes
o   Use textbook CD or website as a resource
o   Predict essay questions
o   Plan and write essay answers
o   Know the structure of the exam (multiple choice, essay, etc.)

Checkpoint

What are some other study methods you use?_____

_____

LEARNING ASSISTANCE AVAILABLE ON YOUR CAMPUS

Do you know what types of learning assistance or academic support are available to you on your campus? Your campus might have a centralized learning center or maybe many tutoring labs scattered throughout the departments on campus. You might also qualify for some specialized assistance through a TRiO program or some other special population program. Your advisor is the best source of information regarding the range of services available on your campus, but here is a brief description of each type of service:

- **Tutoring** (individualized course-specific content tutoring)
- **Supplement Instruction (SI)** and **Peer-Assisted Study Sessions (PASS)** where content is covered for a specific section of a course by an SI/PASS Leader
- **Workshops** on study strategies hosted by a program presented by professional or peer staff
- **Individual Appointments** (this could be about reading, study skills, note-taking or test-taking strategies)
- **Self-Paced Online Tutorials** (covering study strategies through videos, handouts, or quizzes)
- **Support Meetings** with Mentors or Learning Coaches
- **Group Review** for course exams

Hopefully you can see that college campuses are willing and able to help you become academically successful but that you need to take advantage of the services in order to reap the benefits. "Early and often" is a phrase used to explain that you should be seeking help early in the semester and often throughout the semester. Learning assistance doesn't work miracles; you have to put the work in too. Some tips to make the most of the services is to:

- Come prepared with your book and notes,
- Come having made an attempt to solve the problems independently,
- Come being able to identify your questions,
- Come with sufficient time,
- And leave being able to attempt to solve the problems independently in the future.

It is recommended that you change your view of "studying" to "learning" and you think about learning as a multi-sensory experience. You cannot simply read over your notes and learn material (as you see below, you would only be able to retain 10% of what you read); there needs to be more interaction with the material to have comprehension and retention. Look through the Learning Pyramid below to see the average student information retention rates at differing interaction levels.

Learning Pyramid
(average student information retention rates at differing interaction levels)

Retention	Method
5%	Lecture
10%	Reading
20%	Audiovisual
30%	Demonstration
50%	Discussion
75%	Practice Doing
90%	Teach Others

Adapted from National Training Laboratories, Bethel, Maine

Look back at the list of study methods and see where those methods fall on the Learning Pyramid. Think about some study methods you have been using and where those methods would fall in terms of active study strategies that promote better retention of information. Active study strategies can be looked at as effortful learning, just like going to the gym and working out where you are exerting energy to build up strength, you are exerting energy and brainpower to truly learn material. How can you change your study strategies to be more active and efficient to be able to retain more material?

One way to be more efficient in your studying time is by using the study power hour. This has been discussed previously, but studying can also be applied to the hour outline since it is laid out for efficiency. You will start by chunking material into hour increments, which will help you break down your studying into manageable pieces on the front end. For the first 5 minutes, preview the material you will learn during that time and set a purpose. Then spend 40 minutes of studying hard, with no distractions or stopping. Then take a 10-minute break; do something non-academic for those 10 minutes to give your brain a break. Finally, do a 5-minute review of the information you just went over to be sure you understood the material. You might want to test your knowledge of it before you move on, and build a strong foundation before you add more to it. This process can help you draw connections, chunk material so you are not covering too much without going over it, and review material so you are sure you have learned it fully.

Checkpoint

What are the ideal studying habits for you? _____

_____

Why is studying important to your success? _____

_____

What are some ways you can improve your current study habits? _____

_____

STUDY SNAGS

There are many **study barriers** that will decrease your studying efficiency. Here are some quick tips to overcoming some of the most popular study snags.

1. Avoid marathon study sessions.
   After an hour of studying without a break, your brain will not be able to retain any more information. Think of your brain like a muscle — it needs time to rest and become refreshed! For every hour you study, give yourself a 10-minute break!
2. Don't procrastinate or cram when it comes to exams.
   Procrastinating and cramming are not effective with the amount of information you will need to learn and the pace the information is given. Give yourself time to learn the information and get some sleep before an exam!
3. Step away from social media.
   Social media will be there when you are finished studying and you won't miss very much while you aren't looking at it. Social media can be a black hole when you are trying to get things done, so don't use it as a procrastination tool! If you find it hard to self-regulate, try some of the apps that block your access to the Internet, specific websites you tend to spend a lot of time on, or apps that take up a lot of your time.
4. Don't try to multitask while studying.
   Classes you are taking require you to truly learn the information to be able to apply it in discussions, projects, assignments, or tests. When you have to learn more in-depth information, you are not able to move between the information and anything else. Turn off the TV, quiet the music, turn off social media, and stay away from the Internet while studying!

5. Life will get in the way of school sometimes.
   You can't always be healthy, be financially stable, or have healthy relationships with everyone in your life. Life will happen and you can better cope with setbacks if you are prepared!

Checkpoint

What is your study snag? _____

_____

What do you find makes you distracted or inefficient in your time while actually or trying to studying?

_____

_____

LEARNING MODALITIES _____

Have you ever wanted to know why you learn the way you do or why some activities or tasks come so easily while others require more effort? Knowing what makes your mind work the way it does can help you choose study methods that work better for you. Howard Gardner's multiple intelligences theory represents a definition of human nature from a cognitive perspective with seven different ways to demonstrate intellectual ability. Gardner believed that people possess a set of intelligences: intelligence is not a single scalable aspect of a person's style and capability. **Learning modalities** are the sensory means or pathways through which people give, receive, and store information through their intellectual ability. As you might guess, the more senses or modalities we can activate, the more learning will take place, thus referring back to the learning pyramid and multisensory learning.

Want to know how you measure up? Take the Multiple Pathways to Learning inventory on the next pages.

ACTIVITY – MULTIPLE PATHWAYS TO LEARNING _ _ _ _ _

Complete the "Multiple Pathways to Learning" and fill in your scoring grid.

Each intelligence has a set of numbered statements. Consider each statement on its own. Then, on a scale from 1 (lowest) to 4 (highest), rate how closely it matches who you are right now and write that number on the line next to the statement. Finally, total each set of six questions.

1. rarely   2. sometimes   3. usually   4. always

1. _____ I enjoy physical activities.
2. _____ I am uncomfortable sitting still.
3. _____ I prefer to learn through doing.
4. _____ When sitting, I move my legs or hands.
5. _____ I enjoy working with my hands.
6. _____ I like to pace when I'm thinking or studying.
_____ TOTAL FOR BODILY-KINESTHETIC

1. _____ I enjoy telling stories.
2. _____ I like to write.
3. _____ I like to read.
4. _____ I express myself clearly.
5. _____ I am good at negotiating.
6. _____ I like to discuss topics that interest me.
_____ TOTAL FOR VERBAL-LINGUISTIC

1. _____ I use maps easily.
2. _____ I draw pictures/diagrams when explaining ideas.
3. _____ I can assemble items easily from diagrams.
4. _____ I enjoy drawing or photography.
5. _____ I do not like to read long paragraphs.
6. _____ I prefer a drawn map over written directions.
_____ TOTAL FOR VISUAL-SPATIAL

1. _____ I like math in school.
2. _____ I like science.
3. _____ I problem-solve well.
4. _____ I question how things work.
5. _____ I enjoy planning or designing something new.
6. _____ I am able to fix things.
_____ TOTAL FOR LOGICAL-MATHEMATICAL

1. _____ I listen to music.
2. _____ I move my fingers or feet when I hear music.
3. _____ I have good rhythm.
4. _____ I like to sing along with music.
5. _____ People have said I have musical talent.
6. _____ I like to express my ideas through music..
_____ TOTAL FOR MUSICAL

1. _____ I need quiet time to think.
2. _____ I think about issues before I want to talk.
3. _____ I am interested in self-improvement.
4. _____ I understand my thoughts and feelings.
5. _____ I know what I want out of life.
6. _____ I prefer working on projects alone.
_____ TOTAL FOR INTRAPERSONAL

1. _____ I like doing a project with other people.
2. _____ People come to me to help settle conflicts.
3. _____ I like to spend time with friends.
4. _____ I am good at understanding people.
5. _____ I am good at making people feel comfortable.
6. _____ I enjoy helping others.
_____ TOTAL FOR INTERPERSONAL

1. _____ I like to think about how things, ideas, or people fit into categories.
2. _____ I enjoy studying plants, animals, or oceans.
3. _____ I tend to see how things relate to, or are distinct from one another.
4. _____ I think about having a career in the natural sciences.
5. _____ As a child I often played with bugs and leaves.
6. _____ I like to investigate the natural world around me.
_____ TOTAL FOR NATURALISTIC

Scoring grid for Multiple Pathways to Learning

For each intelligence, shade the box in the row that corresponds with the range where your score falls. For example, if you scored 17 in Bodily-Kinesthetic intelligence, you would shade the middle box in that row; if you scored a 13 in Visual-Spatial, you would shade the last box in that row. When you have shaded one box for each row, you will see a "map" of your range of development at a glance.

A score of 20-24 indicates a high level of development in that particular type of intelligence, 14-19 a moderate level, and below 14 an underdeveloped intelligence.

	20-24 (Highly Developed)	14-19 (Moderately Developed)	Below 14 (Underdeveloped)
Bodily-Kinesthetic			
Visual-Spatial			
Verbal-Linguistic			
Logical-Mathematical			
Musical			
Interpersonal			
Intrapersonal			
Naturalistic			

"Multiple Pathways to Learning" from *Keys to Effective Learning*, Sixth Ed., Carter, Bishop, and Kravits (p.33-34).

After filling out the scales and totaling your numbers, determine which of your intelligences are ranked higher than others. Check out the roadmap below to see how your different intelligences shape up against one another and then take a look at the descriptions of the seven multiple intelligences and some quick study techniques that go along with each.

VISUAL-SPATIAL
The ability to conceptualize and manipulate large-scale spatial arrays (e.g., airplane pilot, sailor), or more local forms of space (e.g., architect, chess player).

BODY-KINESTHETIC
The ability to use one's whole body, or parts of the body (like the hands or the mouth), to solve problems or create products (e.g., dancer).

INTRAPERSONAL
Sensitivity to one's own feelings, goals, and anxieties, and the capacity to plan and act in light of one's own traits. Intrapersonal intelligence is not particular to specific careers; rather, it is a goal for every individual in a complex modern society, where one has to make consequential decisions for oneself. (Sometimes called self intelligence.)

MUSICAL
Sensitivity to rhythm, pitch, meter, tone, melody, and timbre. May entail the ability to sing, play musical instruments, and/or compose music (e.g., musical conductor).

VERBAL-LINGUISTIC
Sensitivity to the meaning of words, the order among words, and the sound, rhythms, inflections, and meter of words (e.g., poet). (Sometimes called language intelligence.)

NATURALISTIC
The ability to make consequential distinctions in the world of nature as, for example, between one plant and another, or one cloud formation and another (e.g., taxonomist). (Sometimes called nature intelligence.)

LOGICAL-MATHEMATICAL
The capacity to conceptualize the logical relations among actions or symbols (e.g., mathematicians, scientists). Famed psychologist Jean Piaget believed he was studying the range of intelligences, but he was actually studying logical-mathematical intelligence.

INTERPERSONAL
The ability to interact effectively with others. Sensitivity to others' moods, feelings, temperaments and motivations (e.g., negotiator). (Sometimes called social intelligence.)

 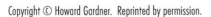

SEVEN INTELLIGENCES

Intelligence	Characteristics	Studying Techniques
Verbal – Linguistic Intelligence	Sensitivity to spoken and written language, the ability to learn languages, and the capacity to use language to accomplish certain goals.	*Limited highlighting, rewriting and outlining information, and discussing information with others.*
Logical – Mathematical Intelligence	The capacity to analyze problems logically, carry out mathematical operations, and investigate issues scientifically.	*Creating graphs and charts, outlining information in a logical progression, analyzing information, and finding patterns in information.*
Musical Intelligence	Involves skill in the performance, composition, and appreciation of musical patterns.	*Studying with music playing in the background, putting information to beats or rhythms, creating rhythm out of words learned, and taking a creative break while studying.*
Bodily – Kinesthetic Intelligence	The potential of using one's whole body or parts of the body to solve problems.	*Moving while studying (pacing while learning new information), moving fingers under words as you read them, and creating flashcards or other items to manipulate.*
Visual – Spatial Intelligence	The potential to recognize and use the patterns of wide space and more confined areas.	*Creating and using visual aids when studying (i.e., graphs, maps, pictures, and color), and trying to visualize information learned.*
Interpersonal Intelligence	The capacity to understand the intentions, motivations, and desires of other people. It allows people to work effectively with others.	*Studying in groups, teaching others information as you learn it, and discussing information with others.*
Intrapersonal Intelligence	The capacity to understand oneself, to appreciate one's feelings, fears, and motivations.	*Visualizing information, keeping a journal, reflecting on personal meaning of ideas, and studying in a quiet place.*

Scenic Overlook _____

Here are some questions to think about in terms of intelligence and it's perception in society.

o   What does it mean to be intelligent in our society?
o   How does society measure a person's intelligence?
o   What abilities do schools value and promote?
o   Do you feel like you relate to your found intelligences? Why or why not?
o   How can you apply your multiple intelligences to your academics?

SUMMARY _____

Studying must involve many different components to be most effective. As you consider your own ways of studying, try to compare them against the study pyramid to see how you can alter what you are already doing well to make it even better. Are you already taking notes? Well, think about a more effective way to take notes so you can use them afterward to study and learn. Not approaching studying in the correct way can result in an inefficient study session. Now that you have seen the attending and reviewing steps in the study pyramid, you can understand why note taking is important to learning. Remember each of the stops you need to make along your way to a test and see how long you need to be at each of those stops to truly learn.

Rev Your Engine

There are many benefits to taking notes by hand and utilizing traditional ways to study, but there are also many benefits to taking notes and studying with technology. New apps and programs are coming out every day to aid you in taking notes and studying for various types of tests. Below are some benefits of taking notes and studying with technology:

o   You can take notes on a variety of mediums.
o   You can access your notes and study materials from multiple devices and from almost anywhere you are.
o   You can be creative in your note taking and interactive with your studying.
o   There is on-the-spot support when you have questions about a topic, by searching the Internet.

Now it's time for you to explore some options in technology you can use for note taking and studying. Answer the following questions as you explore apps and programs:

1.   What are some apps and programs you have found helpful when taking notes or studying?
2.   What are the benefits of using technology to take notes and study?
3.   How can you utilize apps and programs to maximize your note taking and studying?

CITATIONS

Bishop, J., Carter, C., & Kravits, S. (2007). *Keys to College Studying: Becoming an Active Thinker* (2nd ed.). Upper Saddle River, NJ: Prentice Hall.

Carter, C., Bishop, J., & Kravits, S.L. (2011). *Keys to Effective Learning: Study Skills and Habits for Success* (6th ed.). Boston, MA: Pearson Allyn & Bacon.

Dale, E. (1969). *Audio-Visual Methods in Teaching.* New York: Dryden.

Ganly, S. (2010, February 2). *Gardner's Theory on Multiple Intelligences and Study Techniques to Maximize Each Intelligence.* Retrieved from http://voices.yahoo.com/gardners-theory-multiple-intelligences-study-5369465.html?cat=4

Thalheimer, W. (2010). *How Much Do People Forget?* Retrieved from http://www.work-learning.com/catalog.html

Name _____ Date _____

POST TEST/QUIZ

1, What is the average retention rate for those that study in groups?

2. What percentage of material is forgotten 20 minutes after a class?

3. What are 5 study snags?

4. What are the 3 levels of listening?

5. What are the 3 steps in the note taking process?

6. What are 3 note taking methods?

7. What is the total number of intelligences in Howard Gardner's Intelligence Theory?

8. What is the best way to review your notes?

9. What are the 3 areas within the Cornell note taking method?

10. What are the time blocks in the study power hour?

11. Discuss one of your courses and how you can apply the concepts from this chapter.

CHAPTER 6

TEST TAKING: PLAN YOUR ROUTE, ROUTINES, AND REWARDS

By Genevieve Hay

1. **LEARNING OUTCOMES: QUESTIONS TO NAVIGATE**

   a. How should I establish consistent study routines in an environment conducive to successful learning and retention of information?

   b. How do I develop a study schedule and plan that will foster my success in college?

   c. What study and test-taking strategies have I used in the past? Were those strategies effective?

   d. What are study and test-taking strategies that will work best for me?

   e. What are some new study and test-taking strategies that I should consider using?

   f. Are there specific study strategies that are most effective for specific content and levels of learning? What are those strategies?

   g. How do I study for specific types of test items?

   h. How do I combat test anxiety?

   i. What is the value in reviewing a returned test?

   j. How should I plan for exams?

2. KEY CONCEPTS
   a. Personal study environment
   b. Study schedule
   c. Individual versus group studying
   d. Study materials
   e. Study strategies for specific test items
   f. Gardner's assessment and study preferences
   g. Test anxiety strategies
   h. Critical exam review

INTRODUCTION _____

In earlier chapters, you were introduced to a number of critical skills to facilitate your success as a college student. In this chapter, you are now ready to arrange your road trip or study plan. Your road trip will take you through self-testing and to the actual test itself, then on to a critical juncture — reviewing the test after it is returned to you.

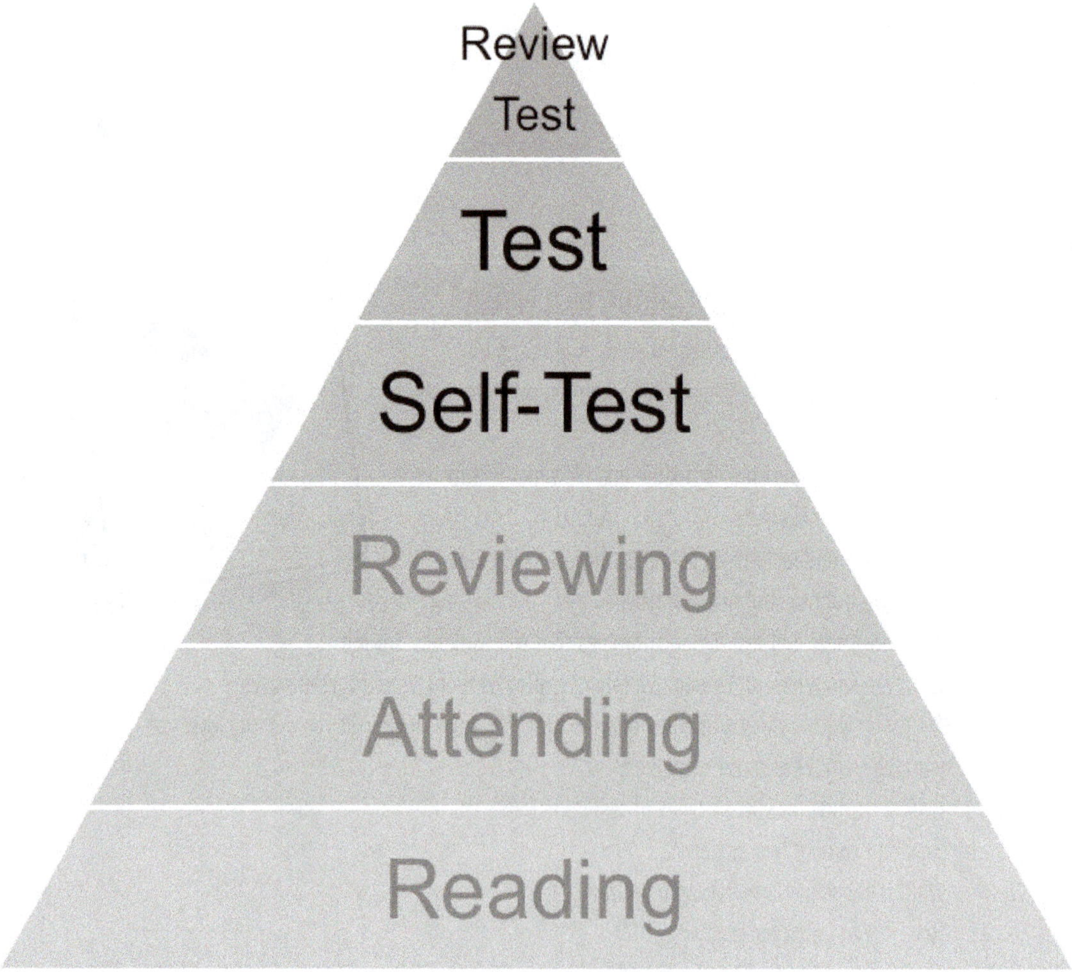

Review

Test

Test

Self-Test

Reviewing

Attending

Reading

Many students find it especially challenging to implement a study plan before taking a test. However, as you think about your study plan, consider how you would plan an important event, like a road trip. Before you take the trip, you would most likely consider the following:

- Where will the travel destination be?
- Who will go on the trip? Should you go alone, with another person, or with a group?
- When will you take the trip? Is there a certain time that would be best? How long would you stay?
- How will you get to your travel destination? Will you travel by air, train, or car?
- What kind of supplies do you need?
- Why is this travel plan the most desired?

Now consider studying for a test, where you will likely face similar decisions and planning in order to have a successful "learning journey." Here are some things you should consider to put an effective study plan in place.

- Who will study with you? Should you study alone, with another person, or with a group of people?
- When will you study? How many days ahead will you need to study? How long should you study each day?
- What kind of supplies will you need, like books, notes, flash cards, and articles?
- Where do you study best?
- Why is the information that you are studying significant?
- How will you approach studying for specific types of tests? How do you learn best?
- How will you deal with test anxiety?

The test preparation information discussed in this section will help you develop an effective study plan before, during, and after you take tests. By consistently using effective study strategies, you will likely find that your grades will improve and you will have deeper and more meaningful learning.

THE WHO, WHAT, WHERE, WHEN, WHY, AND HOW OF STUDYING _ _ _ _ _ _ _ _ _ _ _ _ _ _ _ _ _

WHO should you study with or should you study alone? Based upon what you discovered from your Gardner's multiple intelligences assessment, determine whether studying with others or on your own best meets your learning needs. Keep in mind that your preferences may be different than your classmates'. Also, identify ways to assess whether you are learning through self-assessment strategies. This is especially important if you choose to study alone.

Sample Self-Assessment Strategies (Are you on track or have you veered off course?) One way to ensure that you are on track is to use Cornell Notes (Donohoo, 2011) with a self-test column containing questions related to your notes. Cornell Notes provide a clear study road map and provide you an organized note-taking system along with a cue column to effectively map your study plan, allowing you to check your understanding along the way. As you know, many students find flash cards to be useful study tools. For your personal route, you should decide whether you prefer to use index cards or online resources, like Study Blue or Quizlet. It's also advisable to use questions provided in your textbook or online course quizzes to assess your understanding of course material.

WHAT are you studying?

The first step to prepare for your learning journey prior to a test is to organize all your study materials, such as study guides, readings, lecture notes, Cornell Notes, flashcards, homework assignments, and other relevant class materials, in one place.

WHERE do you study best? (My Personal Study Environment)

While many students study in their rooms, it may be more effective to establish a different location, like the library or an empty classroom, for the sole purpose of studying. CAUTION: SPEED BUMP AHEAD: You should keep in mind that the location you choose should be free from distractions. At many schools, the library often becomes a very social place. If going to the library is the "thing to do" at your school, you may want to look for alternatives or reserve a private study room. After you identify your study location, use it consistently. Be sure your study place is one that you designate solely for studying, which will help set the stage for studying. More than likely, a consistent environment will help trigger your ability to focus and effectively study. Make sure that you have a comfortable chair, ample space to spread out your materials, eliminate distractions, and shut off unneeded technology.

WHEN do you tend to study most efficiently?

Before a road trip, most people figure out the time of day that's best for them to travel. As you know, there are many factors, such as when will you be most alert and/or when you can focus on the road ahead, to consider when traveling. Similarly, determining the time of day you should study requires the same planning. Most important, you need to consider the time of day when you tend to be most alert and when you have completed other essential tasks. Once you have identified your best study time, be sure to schedule study sessions during that time period.

Analyze the Task and Break Down Study Sessions

When you travel, you probably map out your route and decide how far you can travel before you need to take a break. Prior to studying, you will ensure a more successful learning journey and increase your retention by establishing shorter sessions where you study a reasonable amount of material per day. It's important that you be reasonable and specific about what you can learn and that you not cram all of your studying into one major study session on the day before the test. Just like trying to drive too far in one day, cramming will tend to make you fatigued and stressed resulting in a lower than desired grade on the test.

Set Small Study Goals — Stop at a Rest Area When Needed

Like going on a road trip, establish study destination timelines and set small goals to help you break down your study time. In your calendar or journal, keep track of your study habits. This will help you revisit your study routines and determine what's working best for you. As you develop your study habits, it's a good idea to gradually increase your study segments.

For example, if you are reading a textbook chapter, set small goals for the number of pages you will read in a short period of time. If you are solving math problems, identify a limited number of problems that you will solve and check before proceeding to additional problems.

Checkpoint

How have I studied in the past? _____

_____

What are essential components of an effective study plan?

_____

_____

Why it is important to establish a clear and precise study schedule?

_____

_____

WHY is the information you are studying significant?

As you travel, you make plans to visit interesting destinations where you can learn and appreciate the location and culture. Similarly, when you study, consider why the information you are studying is significant. If you can identify the relevance of the material, it will become more meaningful to you. If you can find ways to relate the information to your personal interests and/or goals or apply the information to other classes or real world situations, you will likely be more successful. For example, consider why a specific concept is important and why you should put it on your flashcard or in your notes.

HOW do you study best?

When you took Gardner's multiple intelligences assessment, you were given your learning preference. Have you considered how to apply that knowledge to your study sessions? Could you study with music on? Classical or non-lyrical music is preferred and has been shown to improve performance, known as the "Mozart effect." Could you study outdoors or while working out or walking?

Date _____ Class _____

ACTIVITY: STUDY/TRAVEL PLAN _ _ _ _ _ _ _ _ _ _ _

Test Date - _____

The 5 Ws and How	My Plans
Who will study with me?	☐ Individually ☐ Study partner ☐ Small Group

When and how long do I need to study?	☐ Have I put the test date and study dates in my planner?
	☐ When will I study? How long each day?
	   1 Week Before the Test?
	   3 - 4 Days Before the Test?
	☐ Daily Studying (last 2 days before the test)?

What kind of supplies will I need?	☐ Textbooks ☐ Articles ☐ Cornell Notes ☐ Flash cards ☐ Websites
Where will I study?	☐ Dorm room ☐ Library ☐ Study room
Why is the information that I'm studying significant?	☐ Prerequisite skills/concepts ☐ Key concepts of the discipline ☐ Professional skills/concepts
How will I approach studying for the test? How do I learn best?	☐ Verbal – Linguistic ☐ Logical – Mathematical ☐ Bodily – Kinesthetic ☐ Visual – Spatial ☐ Interpersonal ☐ Intrapersonal ☐ Musical

STUDYING FOR TESTS _ _ _ _ _ _ _ _ _ _ _ _ _ _ _ _ _ _

General Test Preparation Strategies

Prior to a major road trip, careful planning and preparation is essential. Likewise, ensuring a successful test-taking journey begins by preparing for the test as soon as the test date is announced. It's important to anticipate what type of information will be covered on the test and the test format. From there, you can make and implement a study plan and identify and gather all needed materials. To ensure that you are organized and on track for the test, use your calendar and break down studying into smaller, obtainable daily tasks. Plan to actively study by doing things like making and reviewing flashcards, creating study guides, and, perhaps, forming a study group.

Managing Stress and Test Anxiety

Like planning a road trip, some students get anxious as they prepare. You can implement a number of effective strategies to keep your stress level down and to avoid test anxiety. One way to minimize anxiety is to do practice tests in an environment and within the time constraints you will actually have on the day of the test. On the night before the test, be sure to get a full night's sleep. "All-nighters" will make you tired and decrease your ability to focus during the test. It's also important to create a sense of balance while studying — plan for short study breaks that help you relax (i.e., eating healthy meals, exercising, seeing friends, watching television, reading a book, etc.).

It's a good idea to develop study rituals where you identify places where you study best and identify items and study materials that help you study effectively. Be sure to find ways to maintain your concentration by clearing your head, eliminating distractions (like technology, friends, and entertainment) and make sure you have completed all necessary business and put off unnecessary tasks. As you study, provide yourself short study breaks and reward yourself for your accomplishments.

TEST ANXIETY MYTHS

- Students are born with test anxiety.
- Test anxiety cannot be reduced.
- It's bad to have test anxiety.
- Unprepared students will have test anxiety.
- Well-prepared students will not have test anxiety.
- High achieving students and students taking advanced courses will not have test anxiety.
- Attending class and doing homework will eliminate ALL test anxiety.
- It helps to be told to relax when you are anxious about a test.
- Your grades will improve if you reduce test anxiety.

Test anxiety (Akanbi, 2013; Misra & McKean, 2000) is a learned behavior, not a condition. The causes of test anxiety are associated with grades and self-confidence. At times, test anxiety results when one feels a lack of control. Test anxiety can become more pronounced during timed tests. Timed tests can cause the student to fear that they won't finish the test in time even if they know how to answer all the questions or solve all the problems. In order to ease your anxiety throughout the testing process, implement some of the following tips before, during, and after testing.

As you prepare for the test, consider exercising to promote alertness and make sure that you get a good night's sleep on the night before the test. It's also a good idea to eat a snack or a meal before the test. It's not a good idea to go to the exam hungry. On a road trip, having a snack will help keep you going and will help you stay focused. For that reason, you may consider bringing a small snack with you on test day. (Remember — you are able to go further on your road trip if you eat before you depart.)

On test day, you should be able to approach the exam with confidence because you have adequately prepared for the test. To further minimize anxiety, it helps to get to the classroom early and sit in your normal spot or in an area where you can avoid distractions (such as people talking). If you have not crammed, you should find that you will be able to maintain a more relaxed state of concentration. As you travel, it's best to avoid unnecessary conversations that might distract your ability to concentrate on the road ahead. On the day of the test, avoid conversations with classmates who have not prepared or are speaking negatively, as it may distract you as you begin the test.

As you begin the test, carefully read the directions and budget your time for each test section. To help you feel more confident, answer some of the easier questions first. To help you relax, occasionally change your seating position while you take the test. While these efforts to relax may help you on your journey, it is normal to expect some anxiety. Some sense of anxiety can promote a "just right" level of stress to help you make it to your destination successfully.

In order to control your anxiety, consider using some breathing and relaxation techniques. If you go blank, skip the question and go on. If you have time, go back and complete the question. If needed and if allowed, take a break outside the classroom. Be sure to pace yourself during the test and utilize the entire class period to carefully consider each question and to review your work. Finally, disregard students turning in their tests before you. There's no reward for finishing first.

After completing the test, quit thinking about the test and move on to other things. It's best to avoid talking with anyone right after the test to "rehash" it. That may only cause you to question your work unnecessarily. At this point, provide yourself a simple reward (i.e., a cup of coffee, go for a run, read a book, visit a friend) for studying hard and completing the test.

When you receive your graded test, it's important to review your returned test and learn from your mistakes in order to correct them on future tests. However, it's important not to dwell on your mistakes. If these strategies don't alleviate test anxiety, you may benefit from some form of counseling or discussing your preparation strategies with a professional.

Checkpoint

Have you ever experienced test anxiety? _____

What factors contributed to increased anxiety on that test?

_____

_____

How can you avoid or alleviate test anxiety?

_____

_____

TEST-TAKING STRATEGIES _____

In addition to using strategies to decrease anxiety, it's important to use, prepare for, and implement test-taking strategies for specific types of test items, like multiple choice, completion, true/false, and essay questions. In this section, various strategies and suggestions for approaching specific types of test items will be discussed.

During the Test

First, survey your test-taking route, by previewing it quickly to assess the length of the test and to identify the various types of questions. You should determine how much time you will need for each section and type of question. You should provide more time for questions based upon grade weight. Then, carefully read and follow the directions. Make sure to ask your professor for clarification, if needed.

Next, get involved with the test material. Start by answering what you know and be sure to keep a steady pace. If you get stuck, skip and keep moving through the test. If you are allowed to use scrap paper, make a list of the question numbers that you want to revisit later. You might choose to divide this paper into two columns. The first column for the questions you have "No Clue" about and the second column for the questions you "Sort of Know." When you complete the test, revisit the "Sort of Know" questions first, then finish with the "No Clue" group. It is possible that other test questions may provide clues for answering the questions you were unsure about on the first pass. It's also advisable to identify key words and recall what you remember about these terms. Finally, when responding to a question, it's typically best to follow your intuition — your first choice is often right.

When you complete the test, evaluate your work. It's always important to review answers, but don't change them unless you are sure! Look over your test carefully and be sure that you have completed all items and parts of each question. Take into account how test questions are phrased and the origins of the questions. This will help you better prepare for the next tests. (Holzer, Madaus, Bray, & Kehle, 2009)

General Test Taking Tips

As you approach highways and biways, it's important to consider the road ahead and to follow your plan. Similarly, when you approach certain types of test items, you should have a plan in mind. For example, when you respond to multiple choice items, it's a good idea to cover the answer choices, read the question, recall information that you studied, check answer choices one by one, and finally choose the best response to the question. When you approach fill-in-the-blank questions, use the provided terms from the word box. If a word box is not provided, use synonyms for terms if you can't remember the exact term. As you respond to true/false items, remember that if any part of the statement is false, the entire statement is false. Finally, as you contemplate your responses to matching items, it's advisable to look for the easiest items to answer first and read all possibilities each time. By answering the easiest items first, you can use the process of elimination to answer the more difficult items.

Preparing for Objective Tests

Before the Test:
- o Study facts and details. Good tools include flashcards, word lists, mnemonic devices, and chapter summaries. Instead of just memorizing, compare and contrast information on your notecards.
- o Review your notes then close your notes to see how much you recall. (It may help to make a simple exam sheet.)
- o Use online resources provided by your text and quiz yourself.
- o If available, study your old tests.
- o To make learning more meaningful, make real-life connections and apply information that you are learning. Ask yourself the following: "What is the relationship between _____ and _____?" "What does _____ have to do with _____?" "How are _____ and _____ the same/different from each other?" "What is the synonym and/or antonym for _____?" "What are the characteristics of _____ and _____?"
- o Make yourself recall and apply theories at various times in the day.
- o As previously stated, study in small increments over time. It won't help to cram.

Taking Objective Tests

- o Get to the test site early and claim your spot!
- o Stop studying 15 minutes before the test!
- o "Mind dump" any needed information for the test. For example, jot down formulas or key points on the back of the test or in the margins.
- o "Personalize" the test by doing the following. Read the directions for each section and decide what you will work on first and last. Assign times for each section. As you review the questions, separate questions into categories: know, pretty sure, no clue.
  - – Do the questions you know first and don't change your responses.
  - – For the questions you feel pretty sure about, cross out answers you know are wrong. If you still don't know, go back and complete the question later.
  - – For the questions that you have "no clue," cover up the possible answers and answer it in your own words. Then go back through the possible responses and attempt to find the one that best matches what you thought.

Save time at the end of the test to do the questions that you skipped. Utilize information from the other questions to help trigger your memory.

True/False Items

Items to Study for True/False Tests
- o   Key terms, definitions, concepts, and examples
- o   Lists and details
- o   Emphasized points from class
- o   Study guide concepts
- o   Questions from past quizzes and from the end of the chapter

There are certain types of terms that you want to look out for on true/false questions — **absolutes** and **qualifiers**. Watch out for them! Absolute words (no, none, never, always, only, etc.) often indicate false statements. In other words, for the statement to be true, certain conditions must be met 100% of the time. On the other hand, "in between" qualifiers (usually, seldom, many, generally) are often associated with true statements. Look at some examples of these below.

Absolutes

Absolutely	Everything	No
All	Exactly	No one
Always	Exclusively	Nobody
Completely	Forever	No matter what
Definitely	Impossible	None
Every	Invariably	Only
Everybody	Must	Totally
Everyone	Necessarily	Without exception
	Never	

Qualifiers

Almost all	Maybe	Predominantly
Almost	Might	Probably
Commonly	Most	Rarely
Could	No	Seldom
Frequently	Occasionally	Some
Generally	Often	Sometimes
In most instances	On the average	Usually
Many	Perhaps	
May		

Tips for Responding to True/False Items

There are a few other things to keep in mind when responding to true/false items. First, approach long statements with caution! Be sure that all parts of the statement can be supported by your answer. Second, watch out for faulty logic! Some statements may contain an element of truth, but defy logic. For example, "Thomas Edison invented the tickertape machine, and as a result, he became famous." This statement is false, because although he did invent the tickertape machine, he became famous because of his many other inventions. Third, beware of negatives! Read each statement containing negatives carefully. A good practice is to circle all negative words (no, none, not) and words containing negatives (like words with prefixes, like –un, -dis, -in). After circling the words, reread the statement without the negative to determine if the statement is true or false. Add in one negative at a time and keep checking for the truthfulness of the statement. Remember, if one part of the statement is false, the entire statement is false. Assume that a statement is true if there is no word or clue indicating that it is false. Finally, guess intelligently! Look for what you know in the statement and make an informed response.

Preparing for Essay Questions

Essay tests are a form of assessment that allows you to demonstrate whether you have processed and synthesized information from the textbook readings and class discussions. Essay questions require a higher level of understanding and, therefore, require sustained and comprehensive preparation over time. Critical academic survival skills, like attending class, being actively engaged, taking careful notes, and reading the textbook and related course materials, are necessary for success on essay exams. You may consider studying with small groups where you can discuss critical concepts from the course in an informed manner.

As you prepare for essay exams, it's a good idea to do the following. First, it's advisable to predict potential essay questions that might be on the exam. At times, professors will provide possible topics. If so, spend time going through the steps in the writing process (brainstorm, organize, outline, add, support, write, revise, and edit) to develop essay responses prior to taking the exam. As you develop your responses, be sure to include a thesis argument, provide supporting statements, and write a concluding statement. Spend time practicing responses for all potential topics on the exam, within time constraints.

On the exam day, get to class early, bring all needed supplies, and find a comfortable location to work. Prior to beginning the exam, read all directions and writing prompts carefully and develop a brief outline for each question while ideas are fresh in your mind. Assign times for each question allowing time at the end of the exam for editing. Be sure to watch grammar, spelling, and format as you work because you will not likely have time to correct these at the end of the exam. As you complete the exam, re-read the questions and review your responses. Check to be sure you have answered all parts of the questions, you have provided clear points to support your thesis, and that you have provided an introduction and conclusion for each essay.

Below are some examples of different types of essay exam prompts, which are asking you to do very different things. Consider a course you are currently taking and which types of essay exam questions the professor might give.

Essay Exam Prompt Types

Analyze	Be able to separate into parts and show nature, proportion, relationship, and/or effects of relationships between concepts.
Compare	Examine qualities and characteristics to show resemblances between concepts.
Contrast	State dissimilarities or differences of associated concepts.
Criticize	Express judgment as to the merit of a topic being considered.
Define	Give concise and clear meanings of terms. Be able to differentiate between terms.
Discuss	Be able to examine, carefully analyze, and present the pros and cons of a topic.
Enumerate	Be able to list or briefly outline key points.
Evaluate	Be able to present the value or worth of a concept while pointing out both advantages and limitations.
Explain	Be able to clarify and interpret concepts.
Illustrate	Be able to draw, diagram, or graphically represent a concept.
Interpret	Be able to translate and/or explain by example.
Outline	Be able to list main points and supplementary data in a systematic manner.
Prove	Establish your arguments with certainty by providing valid evidence.
Relate	Be able to emphasize connections and associations between concepts.
Review	Be able to concisely discuss and list key points of a concept.
State	Be able to express key points in brief manner.
Summarize	Give main points or facts in a condensed format.
Trace	Be able to give a description of progress or development in sequence.

Checkpoint

What are three study strategies for each specific types of test items?

Objective: _____

_____

True/False: _____

_____

Essay: _____

_____

What tools will you use to study for specific types of test items?

Objective: _____

_____

True/False: _____

_____

Essay: _____

_____

Establish Times When You Will Study for Tests

Using the weekly calendar and schedule that you built and what you've determined to be your best time for studying, establish concentrated periods of time for test preparation. Depending upon the extent of information to be learned, develop a multi-day study schedule prior to the test date. You will learn the information better using distributed study periods over a few days rather than one intensive, cram session. Your planned study sessions should factor in sufficient rest and meals.

Prior to major projects and exams, it's important to develop a long-range study plan with mini due dates to keep yourself on track and to prevent yourself from cramming and doing inadequate work.

Name _____ Date _____

ACTIVITY: PLAN FOR EXAMS (30-DAY PLAN) _ _ _ _ _ _ _ _

The intent of this assignment is to plan for your upcoming exams in a timely fashion. Having a plan can help you stay on track! Complete the template below.

1. Complete the chart below:

Course	Upcoming Paper, Project, etc. Due Dates	Final Exam Date	Material Covered on Exam, Exam Format (Departmental Exam, MC, Essay, Take-Home, etc.)

2. Now complete the calendar below, noting all important due dates, test/exam dates, and time commitments from now until the end of exams:

	SUNDAY	MONDAY	TUESDAY	WEDNESDAY	THURSDAY	FRIDAY	SATURDAY
Wk 1							
Wk 2							
Wk 3							
Wk 4							

3. Working backwards, think about mini-tasks and mini due dates that you can create to help plan for your academic responsibilities from now until the end of exam week.
   - Complete the calendar above with your mini-tasks and mini due dates.
   - Complete your *existing* calendar (on your own computer, in your day planner, etc.) with your mini-tasks and mini due dates.

AFTER THE TEST: CRITICAL TEST REVIEW _ _ _ _ _ _ _ _ _ _

On your journey before this class, what did you do after taking a test? Did you just shove the returned test in your backpack and never look at it again? It is understandable to not want to face a poor test grade but actively using a returned test to learn from your mistakes can ensure better test-taking experiences in the future. It's a good idea to correct old tests and utilize your notes to clarify any misunderstandings that you had.

There are three things that you should do when you receive a test back:

1. complete a critical test review, where you analyze why you were successful with certain responses and why you missed other questions;

2. meet the professor to get help with any problem areas that you had during the test; and

3. consider your study techniques, what worked for you and what did not, then revise your study strategies accordingly.

After your professor returns a graded test, it is important to evaluate your performance to help you improve on remaining tests and assignments for the course. In this section, important steps will be discussed that will help you effectively analyze your performance.

Check the point total to be sure you were awarded all earned points. Ask your professor if you can keep the test or go over it in his/her office so you can re-work the problems/questions you missed. Make sure that you read all comments carefully on essay tests and make notes so you can correct your writing errors before the next test.

It may help to take note of the types of "tricky" questions the professor uses: how can you be better prepared for them on the next test? Try to determine the origins of the questions. Did the question come from the book? Or did the question come from the class notes? Take the time to correct and understand what you missed because you may see it again! Think about the strategies you used to prepare for the test — did they work? What could you do differently next time? Finally, make a plan to start reviewing for the next test at least a week earlier next time. Again, it's important to set times to study in small chunks of time instead of one long cramming session. If you don't understand the errors you made, make an appointment with your professor.

Remember to re-evaluate your ultimate "destination" or grade goal for the semester and determine whether your test score meets that goal. If not, it's time to think about what you should do differently. If you studied alone, you may choose to find a study partner or study group for the next test or consider meeting with an individual tutor or using some form of academic support services to improve your performance.

Critical Test Review

A sound way to review your test performance and to help you enhance your overall performance in a course is to gain an understanding of question types and their levels of difficulty. Bloom's Taxonomy provides categories for levels of understanding that will commonly be used on exams. Knowing the levels of questions will help you determine appropriate study strategies.

When you critically review an exam, you should:

a. Identify the type of question, categorized by Bloom's taxonomy, for each question you missed.

b. Determine which question types you missed the most.

c. Classify each question as to the origin of its information (class, textbook, outside reading or research, lab, etc.).

d. Finally, determine why you missed each question (i.e., careless mistake, did not study that concept, vocabulary term in the question that you did not understand, a concept you thought you understood, test anxiety, etc.). Do you see any pattern? Are there particular kinds of questions that are being missed more often, or is there a common reason for why certain questions were missed?

Once you have analyzed your performance on a test and come to some conclusions, develop and write out a study plan for the remainder of the course. Share your plan with your professor to see if it seems logical. Use the following table to help you gain a better understanding of how to apply Bloom's Taxonomy to your studying.

Skill	Competence	How to enhance studying at this skill level:
Remembering	Recall of basic facts, definitions, dates, events, details, terms.	• Note cards. • Organize information in a table, chart, concept map (Rose, 2011), or outline.
Understanding	Restating in your own words. Understanding and processing information, grasping meaning, applying factual knowledge to a different context.	• To enhance your understanding, it helps to first organize concepts in a meaningful way (outline, table, or concept map). Afterwards, try to teach a study partner the concept from memory. If you are able to discuss the concept easily from memory, you know it. Otherwise, you need to study more! • If you are a visual learner, try drawing your own picture of the concept. Another option is to cover figure or diagram captions from the textbook and write your own caption that explains the figure. Then compare your caption to the one in the textbook. • On an ongoing basis (not just before tests), practice comprehension questions provided in class, online, or in the textbook.
Applying	Using information to solve a problem.	• Do textbook or online practice quizzes and try to identify application type questions. Do you notice any patterns among these questions? If so, that may help you improve your depth of studying and learning. • Develop your own test questions. Share and discuss your questions with your study group. • Textbooks often incorporate introductory and/or concluding essays using key concepts and theories from the chapter in a relevant, real-life manner. Reading and applying what you've learned in the chapter will help you more firmly grasp major concepts. Be sure to discuss the essays with your study group. • Identify key words and concepts (often in bold print or call-out boxes) and research their meanings using an Internet search engine. Hopefully, you will be able to recognize various contexts and applications of the concepts and theories through your research.
Analyzing	Identifying components or parts.	• Do textbook or online practice quizzes and try to identify analysis type questions. Do you notice any patterns among these questions? If so, that may help you improve your depth of studying and learning. • Analyze key terms and phrases of a concept or theory through the use of graphic organizers, like Venn diagrams and concept maps. • Develop and respond to analysis level questions that require you to explain the relationship between theories and concepts. • Be able to explain the significance of a concept and its impact in relation to the discipline being studied.

Evaluating	Relating knowledge from several areas and being able to generalize, predict, or conclude from knowledge and analysis of related concepts or theories.	• Do textbook or online practice quizzes and try to identify evaluating type questions. Do you notice any patterns among these questions? If so, that may help you improve your depth of studying and learning. • Analyze key terms and phrases of a concept or theory through the use of graphic organizers, like Venn diagrams and concept maps. To move to the evaluation level, also make a separate map from another concept or theory. Then put the two maps together and determine connections between the two concepts (i.e., lines and connecting phrases) that clearly show how the two concepts/theories are connected or related to one another.
Creating	Compare and discriminate between ideas; make a decision based on knowledge from information, theories, or concepts. Being able to form a unique thesis, concept, or product.	• With your study group, have each group member write a response to each essay question from the end of chapter or from the online site for the text. Critically evaluate each other's answers and grade them as if you were the course instructor. Discuss your evaluations with you study partners.

Adapted from Alters & Alters, "How to Study Biology," Wiley Student Companion Site.

Checkpoint

Why should I carefully review a returned test? _____

_____

What will I be able to determine from my returned test? _____

_____

SUMMARY

In this chapter, we explored a number of factors that impact your ability to study successfully for tests. You found that it is important to consider study strategies that have and have not worked well for you in the past. Additionally, you were provided opportunities to explore a variety of strategies that you should put in place to improve your ability to study effectively for specific types of tests. Finally, the concept of critically reviewing returned tests was recommended as a means for improving your performance on subsequent tests within the semester.

Name _____ Date _____

ACTIVITY: SEMESTER GOALS _ _ _ _ _ _ _ _ _ _ _ _ _ _ _ _ _ _

After each test you should evaluate your standing to be sure that you are on the right path to getting your goal grade in each course you are taking. So, how are you doing so far this semester?

Class	Current Grade	Goal Grade	Past Due Work	Work Remaining

Rev Your Engine

1. Why not try an app that shuts down your email or Internet while you are studying? Or try to go off of social media for a certain amount of time. How long did you last? What made it challenging?
2. What are some ways you plan to promote a balance of work and relaxation during the semester?

CITATIONS _____

Akanbi, S.T. (2013). Comparisons of test anxiety level of senior secondary school students across gender, year of study, school type and parental educational background. *Ife Center for Psychological Studies/Services*, 21(1), p. 40-54.

Alters & Alters, "How to Study Biology," Wiley Student Companion Site.

Donohoo, J. (2011). Learning how to learn: Cornell notes as an example. *Journal of Adolescent and Adult Literacy*. (54) 3, p. 224-227.

Holzer, M.L., Madaus, J.W., Bray, M.A., & Kehle, T.J. (2009). The test-taking strategy intervention for college students with learning disabilities. *Learning Disabilities Research & Practice*, 24(1), 44–56.

Misra, R. & McKean, M. (2000). College students' academic stress and its relation to their anxiety, time management, and leisure satisfaction. *American Journal of Health Studies*, (16), 1.

Sadler, C.R. (2011). Concept/definition maps to comprehend curriculum content. *The Reading Teacher*, (65) 3, p. 211 – 213.

POST TEST/QUIZ

1. What are critical components of an effective study plan? Describe how you will identify and implement these components for a specific course you are taking this semester.

2. Identify and describe at least three general test preparation strategies.

3. Identify a test preparation strategy for objective test items. Describe at least three considerations to keep in mind when taking objective test items.

4. Identify a test preparation strategy for essay test items. Describe at least three considerations to keep in mind when responding to essay questions during a test.

5. What is test anxiety? What are examples of test anxiety myths? How can someone effectively manage test anxiety? Give several examples.

6. What is critical test review? Why should I carefully review returned tests?

7. How do I use Bloom's Taxonomy to help me prepare for specific types of test questions? Give examples.

CHAPTER 7

DISCOVERING YOUR PATH: MAJOR AND CAREER DECISION-MAKING

By Meredith Gerber

1. **LEARNING OUTCOMES: QUESTIONS TO NAVIGATE**
   a. What are your personal values, skills, and interests?
   b. What role does your major play in determining your career path?
   c. What career planning resources are available to help you research majors and career-related fields?
   d. What is experiential education and how does it play a role in your career success?
   e. What are transferable skills and how can you gain them while in college?
   f. How can you demonstrate knowledge, skills, and abilities on your resumé and cover letter?

2. **KEY CONCEPTS**
   a. Career development process
   b. Self-exploration & assessment
   c. Major vs. career
   d. Career exploration
   e. Informational interviews
   f. Experiential learning
   g. Transferable skills
   h. Targeted resumé & cover letter

INTRODUCTION _____

No matter what your age or academic status, whether you are an 18-year-old freshman or a non-traditional student returning after being away for a few years, it is likely that at some point you have worried about choosing the right major or career (or both!). Perhaps you know what field you want to work in, but you can't decide which major is best or the required courses are proving to be too difficult. Possibly you have chosen a major, but have no idea of what you actually want to do upon graduation. Or maybe… you have no idea about either your major or your career plans (and feel like everyone else has it figured out except you)!

Regardless of where you may be in navigating a route for your major or mapping out your career path, this chapter will provide you with the background to understand how personal values, skills, and interests can be used to make informed major and career decisions, aid in your professional development, and set academic and professional goals. Additionally, you will learn about resources and tools available to assist you throughout the decision-making process.

TIP: Even if you have already made a decision about your major or career, it can still be beneficial for you to read through each section of this chapter. It's not a bad idea to take another look at your intended goals… especially if you're struggling in classes that may be required for you to reach those goals. At the very least, it may give you confidence that you have made the best choice of major or career!

THE CAREER DEVELOPMENT PROCESS

In the past, it was common for people to work for one company, possibly in one position, for the majority of their working lives. However, it is becoming more and more common for people to change jobs and careers multiple times over their work lives. In 2012, the U.S. Bureau of Labor Statistics reported that employees had been with their current employers an average of 4.6 years. While there are a variety of reasons people may change jobs, often it is a result of the reality of the career development process. It is not a one-time choice! **Career development is a life-long process.** That's not to say you will never be satisfied with your career choice, but it may be helpful to know that you're not *stuck* with the choice you make while you're in college.

Consider the career development process to be like the infinity symbol below. You start with **self-exploration** where you identify your skills, interests, personality, and work values through self-assessment. Then you move on to **career exploration** where you will research the field, talk with professionals in that field, and gain some related work experience. But for most people, it doesn't end there…

Self-Exploration:
Skills & Abilities
Interests
Personality
Work Values

Career Exploration:
Research the Field
Talk to Professionals
Work in the Field

Let's say you were considering going into the medical field. You did your research on related majors and careers, spoke with a few doctors or nurses, and then excitedly volunteer in a hospital to gain some experience. But while you are volunteering, you realize you become woozy at the sight of blood or maybe you are having an extremely difficult time with the science courses required for medical school. You would then need to revisit the self-exploration piece, where you will reassess your interests and skills, as well as your major options, which would then lead you to the career exploration piece once again.

Some people are very fortunate and are able to identify an ideal career after very little exploration, but this is not the norm! The majority of people need additional knowledge, time for introspection, and experience to figure out the best fit. If you are still exploring, consider trying a few new classes or volunteering or interning with different organizations to help you research additional ideas. Meet with your academic advisor to discuss your options.

SELF-ASSESSMENT

Have you ever really taken time to assess your values, skills, and interests in relationship to your choice of major and/or career goals? If not, now is the time! (Even if you have in the past, it may be worth your time to take another look to make sure you are still heading in the best direction at this point in time.) The more work you are willing to do now, the more likely you are to make the best decision AND you will have some practice with the process in case you need to go back to the drawing board in the future!

The starting point for choosing your major or career is **self-assessment**. It is better to start by figuring out **who you are and what's important to you, then search for a major and/or career that fits you**… rather than choosing a major or career and trying to fit into it. It is much easier to change your career goals to fit you than changing yourself to fit a specific career. If you know your strengths and skills, activities you enjoy, and what is most important in your life, then you are on much firmer ground to find a major and career that suits you.

You may be asking yourself, "How do I even begin to figure out my values, skills, and interests?!" For most people, when asked, "What do you like?" it can be hard to give more than one or two specific answers. Maybe there are too many things you could list as "likes" or maybe all you can think of are your "dislikes" instead, or possibly you draw a complete blank. However, if you were given a list of subjects, activities, etc. it is usually much easier for you to identify the things you like versus what you don't like, right? On the next few pages you will find a list of potential skills, interests, and values to help you get started.

Read through each section and check all that apply to you. Don't worry too much if you only have a few things checked for a section. Believe it or not, ruling out the things you are not skilled or interested in can be just as useful! This will assist you in narrowing down the long list of options and create a smaller, more realistic list of options you want to spend time researching and exploring (and can help you feel less overwhelmed by all of the possibilities).

Date _____ Class _____

ACTIVITY: SELF-ASSESSMENT _ _ _ _ _ _ _ _ _ _ _ _ _ _ _ _

On the next few pages, you will find a list of many skills, interests, and values. Identify the items that apply to you for each section, then combine and prioritize your results.

Self-Assessment: Functional and Adaptive Skills

Check all skills that apply to you.

ORGANIZATIONAL / INTERPERSONAL SKILLS		PERSONALITY/WORK-STYLE SKILLS
Research	**Communication**	_____ adaptable
_____ question	_____ express	_____ accurate
_____ observe	_____ negotiate	_____ calm
_____ read	_____ persuade	_____ caring
_____ experiment	_____ teach	_____ competitive
_____ analyze	_____ report	_____ concerned
_____ dissect	_____ listen	_____ consistent
_____ synthesize	_____ interview	_____ cooperative
_____ hypothesize	_____ write	_____ creative
_____ use insight	_____ talk	_____ decisive
_____ see relationships	_____ represent others	_____ diplomatic
_____ diagnose	_____ express ideas	_____ efficient
_____ measure	_____ use symbols	_____ empathetic
_____ compare	_____ edit; revise	_____ enthusiastic
_____ reflect	_____ describe feelings	_____ flexible
	_____ perform	_____ foresighted
Manage Information	_____ coach	_____ honest
_____ organize	_____ sell	_____ initiative
_____ account		_____ innovative
_____ catalogue	**Human Service**	_____ insightful
_____ translate	_____ empathize	_____ listener
_____ transcribe	_____ offer support	_____ logical
_____ record keeping	_____ recognize needs	_____ mature
_____ calculate; compute	_____ develop rapport	_____ motivated
_____ create procedures	_____ encourage others	_____ open-minded
_____ compile	_____ establish relationships	_____ patient
_____ systematize	_____ raise self-esteem	_____ perceptive
_____ interpret	_____ help others	_____ persistent
_____ summarize	_____ share	_____ punctual
	_____ accept others	_____ receptive
Managerial	_____ counsel; advise	_____ reliable
_____ manage; lead	_____ mentor; guide	_____ responsible
_____ administer		_____ resourceful
_____ delegate	**Design/Plan**	_____ risk-taker
_____ meet goals	_____ imagine	_____ self-starter
_____ coordinate	_____ conceptualize	_____ sensitive
_____ inspire others	_____ plan; set goals	_____ tactful
_____ enlist help	_____ dream	_____ tolerant
_____ supervise	_____ invent	_____ versatile
_____ make decisions	_____ visualize	
_____ implement	_____ create	

Self-Assessment: Interests

Check the following interests that apply to you.

_____ Accounting	_____ Designing	_____ Law enforcement	_____ Raising funds
_____ Acting	_____ Developing	_____ Libraries	_____ Reading
_____ Administering	_____ Editing	_____ Listening	_____ Recruiting
_____ Advising	_____ Engineering	_____ Machines	_____ Religion
_____ Agriculture	_____ Entertaining	_____ Managing information	_____ Repairing
_____ Analyzing	_____ Entrepreneurship	_____ Making decisions	_____ Researching
_____ Animals	_____ Evaluating	_____ Making policy	_____ Resolving conflicts
_____ Appraising	_____ Film watching	_____ Managing people	_____ Risk (taking)
_____ Architecture	_____ Finance	_____ Medical science	_____ Running
_____ Art	_____ Fine work	_____ Military	_____ Sciences
_____ Assembling	_____ Forestry	_____ Ministry	_____ Selling
_____ Brainstorming	_____ Gardening	_____ Money	_____ Service to others
_____ Building morale	_____ Government	_____ Motivating	_____ Singing
_____ Building things	_____ Graphic arts	_____ Music	_____ Social sciences
_____ Business	_____ Guiding	_____ Negotiating	_____ Solving problems
_____ Challenge	_____ Handling detail	_____ Office management	_____ Sports
_____ Civic activities	_____ Health services	_____ Organizing	_____ Strategy
_____ Clerical work	_____ Helping people	_____ Participating	_____ Supervising
_____ Clothes	_____ History	_____ Performing	_____ Supporting
_____ Coaching	_____ Identifying needs	_____ Philosophy	_____ Systems/procedures
_____ Communications	_____ Implementing	_____ Photography	_____ Teaching
_____ Conceiving ideas	_____ Improving	_____ Physical work	_____ Teamwork
_____ Consulting	_____ Influencing	_____ Planning	_____ Thinking
_____ Cooking	_____ Initiating	_____ Politics	_____ Translating
_____ Coordinating	_____ Installing	_____ Precision work	_____ Transportation
_____ Counseling	_____ Integrating	_____ Procuring	_____ Traveling
_____ Crafts	_____ Interpreting	_____ Production	_____ Unifying
_____ Creating	_____ Inventing	_____ Programming	_____ Volunteering
_____ Cutting costs	_____ Investigating	_____ Promoting	_____ Working outdoors
_____ Data	_____ Laboratory work	_____ Public services	_____ Working with children
_____ Decorating	_____ Languages	_____ Public speaking	_____ Working with objects
_____ Delegating	_____ Law	_____ Publishing/printing	_____ Writing

Self-Assessment: Work Values

The following list of work values describes a variety of satisfactions that people obtain from their jobs. Check those that are most important to you in completing this statement:

I prefer employment that enables me to _____.

_____ Contribute to society	_____ Supervise others
_____ Help others	_____ Have change and variety
_____ Work with people	_____ Work with details
_____ Work with a team	_____ Have stability in my job
_____ Compete with others	_____ Acquire security
_____ Make decisions	_____ Gain recognition
_____ Work under pressure	_____ Experience excitement
_____ Use power and authority	_____ Take risks
_____ Influence others	_____ Make a lot of money
_____ Work alone	_____ Be independent (structure my work)
_____ Be a recognized expert	_____ Live in a preferred location
_____ Be creative	_____ Be self-employed
_____ Acquire new knowledge	_____ Work at my own pace
_____ Contribute to society	_____ Solve problems
_____ Travel	_____ Work indoors
_____ Work outdoors	_____ Work with information
_____ Work with things	_____ Work in the city
_____ Work in a rural area	_____ Live in different locations
_____ Work in the private sector	_____ Work for government or nonprofit

Self-Assessment: Compiling Results

My prioritized list of **Organizational/Interpersonal Skills** (Prioritize your top skills from the list of functional & adaptive skills.)		My prioritized list of **Interests** (Prioritize your top areas of interest from the list of interests.)	
1. _____	6. _____	1. _____	6. _____
2. _____	7. _____	2. _____	7. _____
3. _____	8. _____	3. _____	8. _____
4. _____	9. _____	4. _____	9. _____
5. _____	10. _____	5. _____	10. _____
My prioritized list of **Personality/Work Style Skills** (Prioritize your top skills from the list of personality/work style skills.)		My prioritized list of **Work Values** (Prioritize your top work values that are most important to you.)	
1. _____	4. _____	1. _____	4. _____
2. _____	5. _____	2. _____	5. _____
3. _____	6. _____	3. _____	6. _____

Now that you have a list of the skills, interests, and values that are most important, you should be able to move forward more confidently in choosing your major and/or career. Think about the major you have been pursuing so far: does it match up well with the skills you listed for yourself? What about the career path you have been considering: does it fit well with the interests and work values you identified? Take this list with you to speak with your academic advisor or career counselor. It can be a valuable tool for them to help you work through your major and career choices.

The assessment you just completed is a very basic tool to get you started, but there are many more in-depth assessments that can help you identify your interests, skills, or personality preferences. A career counselor or your campus career center can help you learn about other career assessment tools available to you. Common assessments may include: FOCUS, SIGI 3, iStartStrong, Strong Interest Inventory, Myers-Briggs Type Indicator, StrengthsQuest, and Skills Scan. While there is no magical test that will *tell* you exactly what the best major or career is for you, these tools can assist you in identifying what is most important to you and help you make a choice based on your natural strengths and interests. To get the most out of completing career assessments, follow-up with a career center professional to help you interpret the results.

CHOOSING A MAJOR

From the day you arrive at college, practically all you hear about is the need to choose a major. It seems like all anyone wants to know is, "What's your major?" Not only does the answer determine course requirements, but often your identity in college is linked to your choice of major. In many cases, the people you associate with, the professors you get to know best, and even the clubs you join may revolve around your major.

This seemingly *major* decision may feel pretty overwhelming, especially if you are trying to figure out your career first and then choose the *right* major to match. Many students worry about making the wrong decision and becoming stuck with their choice. You may be asking yourself, "How in the world do I figure out which is the RIGHT major?" The simple answer is this: **the right major is the one you enjoy most AND can do well in academically**. Contrary to popular belief, it's not the one you think has the best career options or highest income potential. If that last statement surprises you, consider this: when students choose a major based solely on perceived career benefits, they may be ignoring the self-exploration piece of the career development process.

Some questions to ask yourself about your choice of major include:

o   Have I taken my skills into consideration? *E.g.: You are planning to be a business major because you want to own your own business, yet math is one subject you haven't been able to successfully pass.*

o   Have I taken my interests into consideration? *E.g.: You are planning to be a communications major because you want to work in the television industry, but you dread writing assignments.*

This isn't intended to discourage you from following through with the major you have chosen or are considering, but it is intended to help you think through the reality of your choice. If you are the student wanting to own a business but struggle with math, you may decide to follow through as a business major, but you will need to be prepared to work even harder to get the grades necessary to graduate. Alternately, if you have already taken multiple business-related courses and are struggling to get passing grades, that doesn't mean you can't be a very successful business owner, having majored in philosophy or art. There is usually more than one path to reach your goal!

Checkpoint

What are my best subject(s) so far? _____

_____

What classes have I enjoyed the most? _____

_____

What do I enjoy doing in my free time?

_____

What skills would I like to develop while in college?

_____

CHOOSING *YOUR* MAJOR _____

Why are you considering your current major? Has someone else suggested you major in education to become a teacher because you are good with children? Or maybe you are skilled in math so others have encouraged you to major in accounting. Are you considering becoming a business major because your parents have told you that there will be more job opportunities when you graduate? Or possibly you don't want to disappoint your family by choosing something that doesn't seem practical (to them).

While your friends and family may have the best of intentions when making suggestions and giving advice, they should not be the only influence on your choice. Remember, YOU are the one who has to attend the classes, complete the assignments, pass the exams, and spend the time studying. Think about it like this: if you were in a position to buy a new car, would you want your family or your friends to pick it out for you? If you are trying to please others with your choice of major, you may be ignoring your own interests, skills, and values, which may set you up for failure. Realistically, if you're not interested in the subject, are you really going to want to study and learn more about it every day? If it's not what makes you happy, it may be time to consider what YOU want to study. Once you make your decision: be confident and trust your choice. (*Consider speaking with your academic advisor or a career counselor if you need help finding the words to assist your family and friends in understanding your choice.*)

> *"Your time is limited, so don't waste it living someone else's life."*
> ~ Steve Jobs

SPEED BUMP _____

Like any good road trip, you may encounter unexpected detours. It is often stressful to realize that your original route (a.k.a. choice of major) is no longer realistic. You may have planned your future around that major for some time and now you feel completely lost! While this may be very uncomfortable and anxiety inducing, it is actually part of your growing and learning experience. Go back to the self-exploration piece of the career development process and continue to learn about yourself. But know that you are not alone in this process. Reach out and ask for help; utilize resources available to you and consult with professionals who know about the career development process.

> *"Alice came to a fork in the road. 'Which road do I take?' she asked.*
> *'Where do you want to go?' responded the Cheshire Cat.*
> *'I don't know,' Alice answered.*
> *'Then,' said the Cat, 'it doesn't matter.'"* ~ Lewis Carroll, *Alice in Wonderland*

THINK YOU'RE IN THE WRONG MAJOR?

By Kate Tiller

You know how sometimes when you are driving somewhere that you have never been, you just get this feeling that you have taken a wrong turn? You feel like somewhere you took a right when you should have taken a left? This is similar to that feeling some people have when they start to examine their academic standing, values, goals, and future plans (as you have been doing throughout this text). Maybe, by this point, you are getting that sinking feeling that you chose the wrong major. What now?

One important point before you get started: If you are a student-athlete or if your institution or your financial aid has specific "progress toward degree" requirements, it is imperative that you speak with the appropriate advisor before changing your major!

Your class standing and number of credits you have toward your current major, along with your institution's rules regarding changing majors, will play a role in how you react to your feelings of uncertainty about your major. Regardless of all of that, the first thing you should do is speak with an academic advisor. You could seek advisement from your current advisor; he may even have insights about how to refocus your current major to better align with your interests. You could also set an appointment with a faculty member in another area of study that interests you to talk about the possibilities of changing to that program. If your institution has a general academic advising office, this might be a good place to start since they can talk with you more generally about all majors. Make sure to talk with an advisor about your course credits and a plan that includes a path to graduation. It is important to know when you plan on graduating and if you have to adjust that plan in order to change your major.

You can also talk with other students who are successful in majors you think might interest you. When you are having these conversations, both with students and advisors, some questions you should ask are: What are the major requirements? Does the major require an internship or a study-abroad experience? What are the students' relationships with faculty like? Of course, you can also do your own research on your institution's website regarding various major options.

The career center on your campus is another place for potential assistance when you are thinking about changing your major. While your major does not necessarily have to be connected to your future career, this department can help you think about what you want to do in the future and map out your plan to get there. Often, this department also provides various career and interest tools that will help you explore your interests and aptitude for certain areas of study. Taking advantage of these services can help you "right your course."

If you have taken multiple classes in a major you no longer plan to (or cannot) complete, all is not lost. Meet with an academic advisor to discuss the possibility of completing a minor in that subject, regardless of your new major choice. (The minor may even complement your new major.) Another possibility is that those courses may simply serve as electives to help you complete your degree. *Note that every major and every college have different requirements; please check with your academic advisor or department for your specific degree requirements.*

Checkpoint

What are your major options?
Locate a list of majors offered by your college and rule out all majors/subjects you are not interested in studying. Once you have eliminated majors, talk with your academic advisor or a career counselor about the remaining majors.

Majors you can definitely rule out:

1.

2.

3.

4.

5.

Majors you definitely want to explore:

1.

2.

3.

4.

5.

Research each major using campus resources, such as department websites, course catalog, and career center resources. Pay particular attention to what courses are required for each potential major. Here are some questions to consider for each major you want to explore:
- o   Are you interested in the majority of the required courses?
- o   What course(s) can you take to help you explore?
- o   Does the department have certain expectations for students in their majors?
    - – Is there a specific GPA requirement?
    - – Will you have to complete a practicum or internship?
    - – Are there clubs/organizations you can join directly related to the major/subject?

MAJOR VS. CAREER

The relationship between majors and careers are not nearly as direct as most people think. While majors such as engineering, nursing, or education can be easily related to particular career fields, most majors provide general academic training not related to specific careers. The basic knowledge and skills developed in a major can be applied to a number of different careers. But, if you are a liberal arts major, never fear… you will not be restricted to only a few career choices!

Your **major choice** should be based on an interest in the subject and the ability to perform well academically in the subject. Your **career choice** should be based on a genuine interest in the work and on having the abilities or skills needed for the work, not necessarily on a particular major. **Choosing a major, then is not the same as choosing a career.** For example, take a look at a typical job description. Very often the employers are asking for specific skills, abilities, or experience — not a specific major! Your major is just one piece of your career path, what you do outside of the classroom can be equally as (and sometimes more) valuable to a potential employer.

Sample Job Description:

We are filling entry-level positions with individuals that have a track record of commitment, ambition, and leadership either through their athletic teams, in their participation in organizations on campus, or in their community. All majors and backgrounds will be considered.

Candidates must represent the following:

- Excellent communication skills

- Leadership experience

- Ability to work in a high-energy environment

- Ambition, strong work ethic, and open to new ideas

- Be a self-starter with problem-solving skills

- Be a career-oriented individual

Majors can relate to careers in one significant way: they help you develop individual skills you can use in a variety of career fields. English majors usually develop or hone their communications skills, especially writing skills. Math and philosophy majors develop analytical and problem-solving skills while history and science majors develop research skills.

NOTABLE NAMES – MAJOR & CAREER

Kenny Chesney, *singer & songwriter* - Advertising
Howard Schultz, *chairman & CEO of Starbucks* - Communications
Diane Sawyer, *broadcast journalist* - English
J.K. Rowling, *author (*Harry Potter *series)* - French & Classics
Martha Stewart, *businesswoman & TV personality* - History
John F. Kennedy, *politician & 35th President of the U.S.* - International Studies
Thomas Jefferson, *author & 3rd President of the U.S.* - Philosophy
John Stewart, *TV host, writer, & director* - Psychology
Dr. Martin Luther King, Jr., *pastor & civil rights activist* - Sociology
Will Ferrell, *actor, producer & writer* - Sports Information
Glenn Close, *actress & producer* - Theater & Anthropology

Checkpoint

Using your campus career center's job board, locate a part-time job, full-time job, or internship posting that you would be interested in applying for (even if you are not qualified at this time). Read through the job description and physically highlight (with a marker or using the highlight feature on your computer) keywords and skills that the employer is looking for in qualified candidates. Does it require a specific degree or major? What types of specific skills are required?

Additional questions to consider:

What skills do I want to gain by the time I graduate?

_____

_____

How can I gain those skills?

    What clubs or organizations can I join to gain those skills?

    _____

    _____

    Are there classes I can take to gain those skills that may also fit into my general education requirements and/or major requirements? Give examples.

    _____

    _____

All of this is not to say that your major cannot play a role in your career choice. The point is that your major does not determine your career options, and vice versa — your career choice does not determine your major options. You could go into a career in marketing with a major in psychology, if you also take advantage of opportunities outside of the classroom that will give you the real-world experience and skills necessary for that career field. Most often you are hired based on the skills and interests you have developed by studying your major, not on the basis of your knowledge about the major. Ultimately, careers are not necessarily determined by majors, but by what you can do and what you want to do!

ACTIVITY: FINDING THE RIGHT FIT _ _ _ _ _ _ _ _ _ _ _ _ _ _

According to psychologist John Holland, people are naturally drawn to work environments where they can utilize their skills and abilities, as well as exercise their personality and values. Therefore your choice of work is often an expression of your personality. He identified six themes in which both our personality preferences and work environments can be categorized: realistic, investigative, artistic, social, enterprising, and conventional. The idea then is that when your personality and work environment theme(s) are similarly matched, the more likely you are to enjoy that type of work.

On the following page you will find "The Party" activity, which will help you learn a little about each of the themes in order to identify the one(s) that resonates with you. While you might find that you identify with more than one theme, typically you can identify two or three that you are more attracted to than others. When you combine those two or three themes, it creates your "Holland Code." For example, you might identify with Realistic, Artistic, and Social. This gives you a code of RAS. As most people have varied interests and are not one-dimensional, occupations often are comprised of multiple themes as well.

Once you have identified your themes/code, work through the pages following "The Party" that include examples of majors coinciding with each theme, as well as sample careers related to each theme. These are not comprehensive lists, so use them as a starting point to generate new ideas or to reinforce that you may be on the right track with your major or career choice. As you read through the lists, write in or circle those you are most interested in exploring further. Then flip to the "Putting the Pieces Together" worksheet to help you organize your thoughts.

Realistic

People who have athletic or mechanical interests and/or ability, prefer to work with objects, machines, tools, plants, animals or be outdoors

People who like to observe, learn, investigate, analyze, evaluation or solve problems - especially those of a scientific nature

Investigative

Conventional

People who like to work with data, information, or numbers; organized in carrying out in detail or following through other's instructions

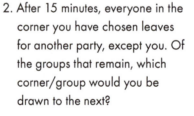
The Party

At this party, people with the same or similar interests have (for some reason) all gathered in the same corner of the room as described here.

People who think up new ideas, have artistic abilities or like to work in unstructured situations using their imagination, inventiveness or creativity

Artistic

People who like to work with people - to influence or persuade them; performing, leading or managing for organizational goals or for economic profit

People who like to work with people - to inform, enlighten, help, train, help them develop skills or cure them; and/or are skilled with words

Enterprising

Social

1. Which corner of the room would you be attracted to, as the group of people who you would most enjoy being with the longest time? Write the letter of that group in the box below:

2. After 15 minutes, everyone in the corner you have chosen leaves for another party, except you. Of the groups that remain, which corner/group would you be drawn to the next?

3. After 15 minutes, this group also leaves for another party. Of the corners/groups remaining, which one of the remaining groups would you enjoy joining?

Majors by Theme

REALISTIC (R)

People who have athletic or mechanical ability, prefer to work with objects,
machines, tools, plants or animals, or to be outdoors.

Typical "Doer" Majors

Agriculture	Fire Science	Marine Biology
Animal Science	Fish and Wildlife Management	Mechanical Engineering
Archaeology	Forestry	Medical Technology
Automotive Services	Heating, Air Conditioning, and Refrigeration	Meteorology
Civil Engineering	Historic Preservation and Community Planning	Military Science
Computer Technology	Horticulture	Natural Resources
Drafting	Industrial Arts Education	Physical Fitness and Training
Earth Science	Landscape Architecture	Plumbing
Electronics	Law Enforcement	Global Logistics &Transportation
Facilities Management		Welding

Majors of interest:

INVESTIGATIVE (I)

People who like to observe, learn, investigate, analyze, evaluate, or solve problems.

Typical "Thinker" Majors

Anthropology	Criminal Justice	Optometry
Astronomy	Data Science	Physical Therapy
Astrophysics	Economics	Physics
Biochemistry	Emergency Health Services	Pre-Dentistry
Biological Sciences	Exercise Science	Pre-Medicine
Botany	Food Science	Psychology
Chemistry	Geography	Science Education
Computer Information Systems	Geology	Sociology
Computer Science	Mathematics	Veterinary Science

Majors of interest:

ARTISTIC (A)

People who have artistic, innovating or intuitional abilities, and like to work in unstructured situations using their imagination and creativity.

Typical "Creator" Majors

Advertising	Dance	Linguistics
Architecture	Design	Communications
Art Education	English	Medical Illustration
Art History	Fashion Merchandising	Music Education
Broadcasting	Foreign Languages	Music
Cinematography	Historic Preservation & Community Planning	Philosophy
Classics	Humanities	Photography
Comparative Literature	International Studies	Studio Arts
Creative Writing	Journalism	Theater Arts

Majors of interest:

SOCIAL (S)

People who like to work with people to enlighten, inform, help, train, or cure them, or are skilled with words.

Typical "Helper" Majors

Athletic Training	Family Studies	Public Health
Child Development	Health Education	Recreation
Counseling	Hearing and Speech	Religious Studies
Communications	Home Economics	Secondary Education
Criminology	Human Services	Social Work
Dietetics/Nutrition	International Studies	Special Education
Early Childhood Education	Middle Education	Substance Abuse Counseling
Elementary Education	Nursing	Urban Studies
ESL Teaching	Occupational Therapy	Women's Studies
Ethnic Studies	Physical Education	

Majors of interest:

ENTERPRISING (E)

People who like to work with people, influencing, persuading, performing, leading, or managing for organizational goals or economic gain.

Typical "Persuader" Majors

Accounting	Hospitality	Pre-Law
Business Administration	Hotel Management	Public Administration
Business Education	Human Resources	Public Relations
Consumer Economics	Insurance	Real Estate
Entrepreneurship	International Business	Restaurant Management
Finance	Management	Retail Merchandising
Global Logistics and Transportation	Marketing	Travel and Tourism
Government	Personnel and Labor Relations	
History	Political Science	

Majors of interest:

CONVENTIONAL (C)

People who like to work with data, have clerical or numerical ability, carry out tasks in detail, or follow through on others' instructions.

Typical "Organizers" Majors

Accounting	Dental Hygiene	Medical Administration
Actuarial Science	Financial Planning	Medical Transcription
Banking and Finance	Food Service Management	Office Systems
Bookkeeping	Hotel, Restaurant, and Institutional Management	Paralegal Studies
Business Education		Purchasing/Materials Management
Computer Programming	Industrial Education	Secretarial Procedures
Computer Systems Operations	Information Systems & Technology	Small Business Operations
Court Reporting	Mathematics Education	Statistics
Data Science	Management Information Systems	

Majors of interest:

Careers by Theme*

	Realistic *Doers*	Investigative *Thinkers*	Artistic *Creators*
Do you like to...?	Repair Plant a garden Build things with hands Operate tools & machinery Play or watch a sport	Think abstractly Observe/question/analyze Solve math problems Perform complex calculations	Sketch/draw/paint/etc. Sing/dance/act Design fashions or interiors Play a musical instrument Write stories/poems/music
Sample Careers	Air conditioning mechanic (RIE) Architectural drafter (RCI) Athletic trainer (RIS) Automotive engineer (RIE) Automotive mechanic (RIE) Baker/Chef (RSE) Carpenter (RA) Coach/referee (RCE) Commercial airline pilot (RIE) Computer/Mathematics Manager (RIC) Construction worker (REC) Dental assistant (RES) Electrical engineer (RIE) Emergency medical tech (RI) Farmer/Rancher (RC) Fiber optics technician (RSE) Firefighter (RIS) Floral designer (RAE) Forester (RIS) Industrial arts teacher (IER) Landscape architect (RAI) Military officer (REC) Optician (REI) Petroleum engineer (RIE) Police officer (RS) Radio/TV repair (REI) Radiologic Technician (RCI) Software technician (RCI) Truck driver (RSE) Welder (RE)	Actuary (ISE) Anesthesiologist (IRS) Anthropologist (IRE) Archaeologist (IRE) Biochemist (IRS) Biologist (ISR) Chemical engineer (IRE) Chemical technician (IRE) Chiropractor (IRS) Computer analyst (IER) Computer programmer (IRC) Coroner (ICR) Dentist (ISR) Dietician (IES) Ecologist (IRE) Economist (IAS) Geologist (IRE) Historian (IA) Horticulturist (IRS) Medical technologist (ISA) Meteorologist (IRS) Nurse practitioner (ISA) Pharmacist (ICE) Physician (ISE) Physician assistant (ISA) Psychologist (IES) Respiratory Therapist (IRS) Science teacher (IRS) Statistician (IRE) Technical Writer (IRS) University professor (IAR) Urban planner (IE) Veterinarian (IRS)	Actor (AES) Advertising art director (AES) Advertising manager (ASE) Architect (ARI) Artist (A) Art Teacher (ASE) Attorney (A) Clothing designer (ASR) Copywriter (ASI) Choreographer (ASE) Dancer (AES) Drama teacher (ASE) Editor (ASE) Entertainer/performer (AES) English teacher (ASE) Fashion designer (ASR) Fashion illustrator (ASR) Furniture designer (AES) Graphic designer (AES) Interior designer (AES) Journalist (ASE) Landscape Architect (AIR) Librarian (A) Medical illustrator (AIE) Museum curator (AES) Musician (AE) Music teacher (ASE) Photographer (AES) Producer (AES) Set designer (AR) Theatre/movie/television director (AES)

*Circle any of the sample careers you are interested in exploring further.

Careers by Theme*

	Social *Helpers*	Enterprising *Persuaders*	Conventional *Organizers*
Do you like to...?	Teach/train others Express yourself clearly Lead a group discussion Mediate disputes Cooperate well with others	Initiate projects Persuade people Sell things/promote ideas Organize activities Lead a group	Work well within a system Organized Keep accurate records Work with numbers Attention to details

Sample Careers	Animal trainer (SRE)
	Athletic coach (SRE)
	Chaplain (SAI)
	Clinical dietitian (SIE)
	College instructor (SA)
	Community organization
	  director (SEA)
	Counselor (SAE)
	Dental hygienist (SAI)
	Elementary school
	  teacher (S)
	Historian (SEI)
	Hospital administrator (SER)
	Mail carrier (SRC)
	Medical records
	  administrator (SIE)
	Minister/priest/rabbi (SAI)
	Nurse (SIR)
	Occupational therapist (SAR)
	Real estate appraiser (SCE)
	Recreation therapist (SA)
	Park naturalist (SRI)
	Parks & recreation
	  manager (SE)
	Physical therapist (SIR)
	School administrator (SEA)
	Social worker (SEA)
	Special education teacher
	  (SAI)
	Speech pathologist (SAI)
	Volunteer services director
	  (SEC)
	Youth services worker (SEC)
		Advertising executive (ESA)
		Automobile sales person
		  (ESR)
		Buyer (EC)
		Chef (EA)
		Claims adjuster (ESR)
		Computer operator (ESI)
		Cosmetologist (ECA)
		Credit manager (ERS)
		Dental assistant (E)
		Education & training manager
		  (EIS)
		Elected public official (EAS)
		Flight attendant (EAS)
		Hotel manager (ESR)
		Human resources manager
		  (EAS)
		Insurance manager (ESC)
		Interior designer (EA)
		Interpreter (ESA)
		Investments manager (EIR)
		Lobbyist (ESA)
		Marketing manager (EA)
		Optician (ECR)
		Personnel recruiter (ESR)
		Public relations rep (EAS)
		Realtor (E)
		Restaurant manager (ECR)
		Retail sales rep (E)
		Sales manager (E)
		Stockbroker (ESI)
		Top executive (E)
		Travel consultant (ECA)
			Air traffic controller (CRE)
			Accountant (CSE)
			Actuary (CI)
			Administrative assistant (CS)
			Bank teller (CSE)
			Bookkeeper (C)
			Budget analyst (CER)
			Building inspector (CSE)
			Business teacher (CSE)
			Cartographer (CRI)
			Computer system analyst (C)
			Court reporter (CSE)
			Credit manager (CE)
			Customs inspector (CER)
			Editorial assistant (CSI)
			Farmer/rancher (CSE)
			Financial analyst (CSI)
			Financial manager (CE)
			Forensic specialist (CRI)
			Food service manager (CES)
			Health information
			  specialist (C)
			Insurance underwriter (CSE)
			Legal secretary (CSA)
			Math teacher (CIR)
			Medical records tech (CSE)
			Military enlisted (CRE)
			Museum registrar (CSE)
			Nursing home administrator
			  (CES)
			Paralegal (CE)
			Pharmacy technician (CR)
			Tax consultant (CES)

*Circle any of the sample careers you are interested in exploring further.

Putting the Pieces Together

DIRECTIONS: After you have identified your three themes from "The Party" worksheet, list each theme in the first column. Next, select your top three majors from each theme you identified on the "Majors by Theme" worksheet and write them beside the corresponding theme in the second column. Finally, select your top three occupations from the "Sample Careers" for each of the three themes found on the "Careers by Theme" worksheet and write them in the third column.

Themes	Majors	Careers
	1. 2. 3.	1. 2. 3.
	1. 2. 3.	1. 2. 3.
	1. 2. 3.	1. 2. 3.

Now what?

Step 1: Research majors at your college by reviewing the department websites, reading your course catalog, meeting with a faculty advisor in the department, and speaking with current students in those majors.

Step 2: Take courses to explore possible majors. Meet with your academic advisor to discuss which courses will give you the best introduction.

Step 3: Declare your major! (Check with your academic advisor to learn how this is done at your college.)

Step 4: Research careers on O*Net (http://online.onetcenter.org) and using additional resources on your career center's website. Conduct informational interviews with professionals, alumni, friends, relatives, etc. to learn more about certain industries, career paths, and graduate schools.

Step 5: Explore careers and gain experience by shadowing a professional, volunteering, working part-time, or through an internship.

*Scenic Overlook*_____

Now that you have started to identify your skills, interests, and values, take a moment to think about what you have learned about yourself. Was there one area of interest or skill that stands out as being most important? Were there any results that surprised you? How might your themes impact your choice of major? Your choice of career? What are your next steps?

MAJOR & CAREER RESEARCH _____

Now that you have identified a few potential majors and/or careers, it's time to begin the fun part — research! There are a number of resources readily available to you.

Major Research

As previously mentioned, researching majors starts with learning about the options available to you at your college by reviewing the department websites, reading your course catalog, meeting with a faculty advisor in the department, and speaking with current students in those majors. Additionally, you will want to take courses to explore majors, meet with your academic advisor to discuss which courses will give you the best introduction, and finally you will be ready to declare your major!

But what if your college doesn't offer a major(s) that you identified through "The Party" exercise? Go to your academic advisor to find out if there are majors and minors that you could combine to help you gain the same knowledge and skills. If that is still not an option, you may need to look at other colleges, community colleges, or technical schools for those majors.

Career Research: Where to begin?

Start with your career center's website. Look for links to online resources such as:
o   O*Net (http://www.onetonline.org/)
o   Occupational Outlook Handbook (http://www.bls.gov/ooh/)
o   "What Can I Do With This Major?" (http://whatcanidowiththismajor.com)
o   And others that describe a variety of career fields, educational requirements, salary ranges, and the employment outlook.
o   LinkedIn.com is another resource for collecting information on career fields as well as networking and resumé sharing. Explore the LinkedIn site to see if your college and/or career center has an alumni group that you can join.

Attend talks and presentations about careers. Often your campus career center and/or major departments will invite guest speakers to discuss their career paths. This is a great opportunity to learn more about their path and gain advice about what you can do to be prepared for a similar career. It's also an opportunity to meet people in a particular field of interest.

Speak with friends, family, alumni, and others currently in your career field of interest. This is called **informational interviewing**. Informational interviewing is an opportunity for you to gather information from professionals in a specific industry about the skills, experience, and training required for their career field. These interactions can be formal or informal; it depends on your familiarity with the person you are interviewing. If you are speaking with alumni or someone you were referred to, treat this as a more formal meeting. Informational interviewing is also a great way to start building your professional network. A network will be extremely important once you start looking for jobs.

What to do first:
- Plan out what you want to say either on the phone or in an email. (This will help you be less nervous.)
- If you are contacting a referral from a friend or family member, be sure to mention the name of the person who referred you.
- Mention that you only need about 20 minutes of his/her time for the informational interview.
- Ideally you will want to ask for a personal interview as opposed to email or phone.

What to ask:
- Ask how the person got started, what they like and don't like about their job, company, or industry.
- Ask about career opportunities in the field, such as internships, entry-level jobs, etc. and whom you should contact about those potential opportunities. (*But do NOT ask for an internship or job! Remember, you're just gathering information.*)
- Ask open-ended questions (not Yes/No), such as:
  - How did college prepare you for this job?
  - Where do you see the industry heading in the next few years?
  - What do you like (dislike) about your job or organization? Why?
  - What is a typical career path in this field?
  - What are typical entry-level positions in your field?
  - What skills and experience are necessary?
  - Is there anything else I should know about this field/industry?
  - Who else would you recommend I speak to for advice in this field?

During the interview:
- Be organized! Keep records, including the date of every contact you make with every person.
- Take notes! You may want or need to refer back to something mentioned in the interview. It will also give the impression that the information is important to you. (Don't forget to take your list of questions along with you!)

After the interview:
- *Send a thank you note immediately after the interview.* This can be either handwritten or via email. (But so few people still hand-write letters that it may be more appreciated if you have the time and desire to do so!) Personalize the letter by referencing something that you all discussed or a notable or helpful part of the conversation.
- *Contact people referred to you by the person you interviewed.* Make sure to mention the mutual contact that referred you, as well as why he/she thought this new contact might be helpful.
- *Stay in touch!* Keep your contacts informed. If the original contact referred you to someone who was helpful, send him/her a quick note with that information. Networking contacts are often sincerely interested in helping if they can and are curious about what happens in your career adventure.

Checkpoint

After conducting an informational interview(s), consider the following:

What did you discover?

_____

What knowledge or resources did you gain?

_____

Does the major/career field fit you? (Consider your skills, interests, and values.)

_____

What did or didn't interest you about the major/field?

_____

What more do you need to know?

_____

Scenic Overlook

Consider whether you can:
o Narrow your potential major or career options after having done this research?
o Create list of steps to reach your goal?
   o Identify your end goal & work backwards to create a list. *E.g.: Does the career field require graduate school, certification, or specific work experience? How/when will you need to complete or earn the degree or experience? When do you need to begin each part?*
   o Identify your short-term goals vs. long-term goals. *E.g.: What needs to be done/completed in the near or immediate future? What can be done/completed later?*

NEXT STOP: EXPERIENTIAL LEARNING _____

Once you have narrowed your choices down to one or two career fields you really want to explore, the next step is to take it for a test drive, get your feet wet (also known as, experiential learning)! **Experiential learning** is a hands-on approach and provides a chance for you to *learn* through *doing*. This can be a great opportunity for you to learn new skills and sharpen skills you already possess. It may also help you combine some of what you've been learning in the classroom with real-world experience!

Need more reasons why you should take advantage of experiential learning? It helps you:

o   Gain "real-world" exposure to a specific industry.
o   Explore what you can do with your major, skills, and interests.
o   Test drive your career choices and options before committing to a job or specific industry.
o   Build your resumé.
o   Make professional contacts in your field of interest (networking).
o   Distinguish yourself from the competition.

There are many ways for you to gain experience. The most common types of experiential learning opportunities are:

Internships

Internships allow you to work in a structured, supervised professional environment where you can gain practical experience. There should be intentional learning goals and objectives, and you (as the intern) must actively reflect on what you are learning throughout the experience. You will need to speak with your major advisor to learn if you are able to earn credit for an internship (some majors will require it). But don't worry if you can't earn credit, there are plenty of wonderful non-credit-bearing internship opportunities! And know that it's never too early to start gaining internship experience — you don't need to wait until your junior or senior year to explore. Go to your career center to speak with someone about how to find available opportunities or how to create them.

Part-time Job

Don't think of getting a part-time job just to earn money (although money is nice and often a necessity). Think of it as a way to test out a career field AND earn money! Look for jobs that are in an industry that you have researched. For example, if you want to go into healthcare, consider getting a part-time job in a medical office. Even if you are filing papers and charts, you are still experiencing a medical work environment, hearing the terminology used, and getting a sense of what the day-to-day activities look like for a variety of positions within that office. It's also a great way to build that network of professionals that may be useful later when you're searching for jobs or applying to graduate school. While career-related part-time jobs don't offer the same structure and supervision of an internship, it can still be equally as valuable.

Job Shadowing

You may have already done a bit of job shadowing in high school or on your own. But if you're not familiar with the term, it refers to short-term observation of professionals in a career field of interest to you. If you were considering going into law, you may be able to sit in the courtroom and experience what an average day is like for lawyers, judges, and other staff. Like internships and part-time jobs, it gives you some insight into what skills are required, typical tasks you might be expected to complete, and a sense of what the work environment feels like in reality.

Undergraduate Research

Students who want to pursue a career in academic or science-related fields will want to assist in, or conduct, research as an undergraduate. Often your major department will have faculty members who are already conducting research and are in need of students to help. This is a great opportunity for you to work closely with a faculty member in their field of expertise, learn about what is trending in that field, as well as (once again) growing your professional network.

Volunteer/Service Learning

Your good intentions to get involved in the community or to support a service organization can be beneficial to your career as well. This can be especially true if you look for opportunities that allow you to utilize your skills to benefit a community or organization and/or if you are able to gain new skills as a result of your volunteer efforts. For example, you may have a love for children and are interested in finance as a career field. You could volunteer to assist the accountant or the fundraising director for an organization that serves impoverished children. However, don't just volunteer for 10 different organizations where you might be handing out water or snacks at a one-time race. Make your volunteer experience meaningful and intentional. Once again, this is providing a chance for you to grow your professional network — and who knows, you may find an interesting new career path through the experience!

Study Abroad

If you're able to take advantage of studying abroad, you can gain key skills such as adaptability, leadership, language proficiency, communication, and independence. You may even find that you return more confident and mature. *All of these are valuable and transferrable skills sought after by employers.* Additionally, if you have the option to work part-time or intern while abroad, you're gaining a global perspective of the world of work. Who knows, you may even end up making a career connection that will be beneficial when looking for a job after graduation.

Student Activities

You might have joined clubs or organizations on campus to meet like-minded students, but you can also gain career-related experience and skills. Look for opportunities within the group(s) to try out or practice a skill or area of interest. If you're considering a career in marketing, volunteer to help with making flyers and advertising club events, or better yet — become the marketing chairperson! Or maybe you are considering a career in finance; look into becoming the treasurer or help with collecting membership dues to test it out. A few of the common skills you could walk away with are communication, teamwork, and leadership.

Regardless of whether you try one or all of the experiential learning opportunities mentioned above, you will hopefully walk away from the experience(s) with more information about possible career fields, new or additional skills to make you more marketable, and new contacts to add to your professional network! At the very least, you may be able to rule out a career field or learn something new about how to work with different personalities and/or supervision styles.

Checkpoint

After completing one of the above experiential learning opportunities, ask yourself the following questions:

- o What did you observe, learn, or experience during your internship, part-time job, etc.?
- o What was the most meaningful part of the experience?
- o Was there anything you experienced that was unexpected (positive or negative)? How/why was it different than you expected?
- o Did this experience help you confirm or rule out this as a possible career path? How/why did it confirm/rule out possibilities?
- o What is your next step? Do you need to:
  - o Try another opportunity in the same field to gather more information?
  - o Regroup and try another career field?

Transferable Skills

Many graduates, especially liberal arts graduates, get hired because of their experience, skills, and interest in a career field, not necessarily on the basis of a major. As described in the previous sections, there are many ways for you to gain and hone your skills. Perspective employers want you to be able to apply the skills you have learned through your education, work, and life experiences to the work environment. In other words, they are interested in your **transferable skills**; skills that you have gained and can apply to the job they want you to do.

According to the 2014 National Association of Colleges and Employers (NACE) Job Outlook survey, the top 10 skills and qualities employers want are *transferable skills*:

1. Ability to work in *teams*
2. Ability to *make decisions and solve problems*
3. Ability to *plan, organize, and prioritize work*
4. Ability to *verbally communicate*
5. Ability to *obtain and process information*
6. Ability to *analyze quantitative data*
7. *Technical knowledge* related to the job
8. Proficiency with *computer software programs*
9. Ability to *create and/or edit written reports*
10. Ability to *sell or influence others*

Similar to the challenge of identifying your interests, it can be difficult for people to identify their skills as well. On the following pages you will find a list of a wide variety of transferable skills. Use the worksheet to help you think through the skills you have developed or need to develop to reach your career goals. Then describe how you developed the skill or how you will go about developing that skill. You may be surprised to find that you have multiple examples of how you have developed or could develop a specific skill.

Transferable Skills	Developed (have this)	To Develop (need this)	How did or How will I develop this?
Communication Skills			
Oral – speaking effectively			
Written – being clear and concise			
Listening Objectively – able to paraphrase			
Decision Making & Problem Solving Skills			
Problem Solving – developing solutions			
Critical Thinking – thinking outside the box			
Foresight – anticipation, needs assessment			
Reasoning – forming conclusions, inferences or judgments			
Identifying Issues – apply criteria, analyzing & interpreting			
Management & Administration Skills			
Leadership – setting an example			
Motivation – inspiring others			
Delegation – identifying & selecting people for tasks			
Budgeting – allocation of assets			
Conduct Meetings – negotiating, mediating			
Presentation – ability to use various media			
Research & Investigation Skills			
Identifying problems, needs, and solutions			
Designing Experiments – testing & validating data			
Technology – use & knowledge of a variety of sources			
Evaluations – developing questionnaires & models			
Laboratory Techniques – proper use of			
Interpersonal/Human Relations Skills			
Networking – developing interactions with others			
Team Player – appreciating contributions of others			
Empathic – generating understanding & trust			
Tact – expressing one's self appropriately			
Diplomacy – ability to deal with others			

Transferable Skills	Developed (have this)	To Develop (need this)	How did or How will I develop this?
Flexibility Skills			
Creative – originality & expressiveness			
Innovation – unique ways of solving different problems			
Adaptable – accommodating & seeing alternatives			
Conceptualize – deriving ideas from inferences			
Information Management Skills			
Synthesize – organize facts, concepts, & principles			
Catalog – compile, rank, & itemize information			
Manipulate Information – evaluate against appropriate standards			
Computer Knowledge – understanding & using software			
Sorting – data & objectives			
Planning & Organizing Skills			
Effective time, energy, & resource management			
Visualization – predicting future trends & patterns			
Initiation – implementing projects & ideas			
Scheduling – setting & reaching goals			
Prioritizing – arranging according to importance			
Accountability – follow through with plan or decision			
Dimensional Sight – illustrating, displaying, & creating			
Personal Development Skills			
Motivated – going beyond the expected			
Commitment – deciding for the common good			
Independence – working without guidance			
Confidence – having a positive personal attitude			
Poise – composure; free from affection; balanced			
Energy – displayed enthusiasm			
Knowledge – proficiency in field of study			

What did you learn about yourself through this exercise?

_____

_____

Do you have more skills than you originally expected? Were there any that surprised you?
Which ones and why?

_____

_____

Are there any skills you currently possess but feel you need to develop further? Why?
How will you develop them?

_____

_____

Have you compared your skills to the career field of interest? Are there any new skills to add to your list
to develop after this comparison?

_____

_____

What is your next step for the skills you want or need to develop? Can you identify classes or
experiential learning opportunities that will help?

_____

_____

Which skills would you enjoy using the most?

_____

_____

What are *your* top 10 transferable skills?

1. _____   6. _____

2. _____   7. _____

3. _____   8. _____

4. _____   9. _____

5. _____   10. _____

Not only can identifying your skills help you explore your career options, but it can also help you prepare for your job or internship search, as well as interviewing. So take note of your strongest, most well-developed skills and make sure you can talk about them and/or describe them to others. Additionally, you can use this worksheet to help you with the next section, building a resumé.

RESUMÉ AND COVER LETTER_____

Throughout this chapter you have been exploring your interests, values, and skills and how they relate to your major and career choice. Now it is time to create documents that help others understand how all of those things shape who you are, what you've done, and how it relates to a potential job. Your resumé and cover letter help you paint a picture of those skills, accomplishments, and experiences for a potential employer — not just full-time or part-time employers, but for potential internship supervisors, volunteer coordinators, graduate school admissions, etc.

What is a resumé?

A **resum**é is a *brief* summary of your skills, strengths, accomplishments, and your work-related history. Think of it as a selling or marketing tool to help you get an interview. Very often this will be an employer's first introduction to you as a potential employee. *The purpose of it is to secure an interview, not to get the job!*

You may have created a resumé in high school, listing everything you've ever done, but now that you're in college, your resumé should look very different. *And for those of you who are not recent high school graduates, this advice is for you, too!* Too often resumés are ineffective because they are just a running tally of every job, every club, and every honor or award you ever received. Do you really think employers have time to read your three-page resumé when they have a stack of 100 resumés to review? Not likely — especially when you consider that employers spend about 20-30 seconds scanning a resumé. So you may be wondering, "What *should* I include?"

Unfortunately, there is no definitive answer to the above question. What you should (or should not include) truly boils down to how you intend to use the resumé. Contrary to popular belief, there is no one-size-fits-all resumé and no real need for a *general* resumé any longer. You will most likely have multiple versions of your resumé based on what you apply for or how it is being used. This is known as a **targeted resum**é. For example, you may have one version that you will use to apply for a scholarship or to graduate school that highlights your academic accomplishments and a completely different one that you use to apply for a marketing internship that highlights your related skills and experience. Targeted resumés are much more useful to your reader/potential employer and allow you to showcase your experience that is most similar to or related to the job, internship, or other opportunity.

Your best bet when applying for jobs or internships is to first read the job description carefully to identify the skills, qualities, and/or experience that they are looking for in candidates who apply for the position. Once you have an idea of what they want versus what you have to offer, then you can begin to develop an effective and targeted resumé.

Here are a few tips of what you may want to consider while working on your resumé:

1. **Highlight your achievements, skills, and what you have learned.** Don't just list duties you performed, but tell your reader what you gained or learned through the experience. Include those that are most relevant to the job/internship at the beginning of your resumé.

2. **Don't undersell yourself!** Many students will not consider part-time jobs, volunteer experiences, class projects, or student organizations as relevant information when applying for professional jobs/internships. Most likely your involvement in those experiences helped you learn/hone skills or gain knowledge, so include those that are relevant.

3. **Be concise.** Keep your resumé simple and to the point, so that an employer can read over it quickly (remember the average is 20-30 seconds).

4. **Quantify your experience when possible.** For example, instead of "Tutored students" write "Tutored three Spanish 101 students 2-3 times per week during the fall semester."

5. **Be consistent.** Make sure the order of information provided, formatting (fonts, bullets, spacing), and highlighting is consistent throughout your resumé.

6. **Use action verbs to describe your skills and experience.** Instead of "Responsible for preparing…" use "Assisted in preparing…" or "Prepared…"

7. **Check your grammar and spelling.** Don't just rely on your computer's spell/grammar check feature. Ask at least one other person to proofread your resumé. (Ideally, ask more than one person to read it!)

8. **Keep it to one page.** Refer to #3 above. It is not likely that an employer will make it to that second or third page in 20-30 seconds. Eventually, if you have a great deal of experience and related skills, you may have more than one page. But for now, keep it short and sweet.

The following pages comprise suggested items to include on your resumé and a sample resumé. As mentioned above, there is no one *right* way to do a resumé, but it may help to see an example of what others have done. Then you can pick and choose the aspects you want to incorporate into your own resumé. Ultimately, ask yourself if it gives the first impression you want it to give someone you may have never met, is it a good representation of yourself, and most important, are YOU happy with it?

SUGGESTIONS OF WHAT TO INCLUDE _ _ _ _ _ _ _ _ _ _ _

Your full name (*in all capital letters and/or bold*)
Complete address (*list permanent and present addresses if in college*)
Home and/or mobile phone numbers
Email address (*Make sure your email address does not sound unprofessional*)

OBJECTIVE

The career objective* tells an employer how you fit in the organization. It forces you to focus on your job interest, and it unifies the rest of your resumé. Three pieces of information make up the objective:

1. The level or type of position (example: entry level, sales trainee, social worker)
2. Where the job is located in the organization or industry (example: international news, marketing department)
3. Interests, knowledge, or skills you wish to share or hope to incorporate into your work

Example: "To obtain an entry-level position in human resource management with particular interests in wage and salary administration."

* *Objectives are optional, but if you choose to use one, it needs to be specific to each individual job, internship, etc.*

EDUCATION

This section may contain the following: **names and locations of schools** or programs; **graduation date** (or expected date); **degrees, certificates, or licenses**; **major**; **grade point average** IF 3.0 or above; **coursework** related to the job you want; **awards or scholarships**; and/or, **study abroad experiences**. These may also be separate sections in your resumé.

EXPERIENCE

Be sure that you cover full-time, part-time, internships, volunteer work, military service, and self-employment. However, it is not necessary to list every job you've ever had. If you have had a lot of work experience, limit the jobs you list to the three or four you consider the most important as learning experiences. Include your **job title**; **employer name** (company or organization); **city/state**; **dates of employment; and bulleted, active descriptions of your responsibilities and major accomplishments.**

ACTIVITIES, HONORS, AND/OR SKILLS

You may want to mention **interests and activities that demonstrate job-related skills** (leadership, organization, etc.); **special abilities,** such as knowledge of computers or a foreign language; and/or **honors or awards earned**. Do not include personal data, such as age and health status.

REFERENCES

You can indicate that references are available upon request (if there is space), but do not list them on your resumé. Then list 3-5 references on a *separate page* that is the same type of paper as your resumé.

P.R. Society

14 Any Street, Your Town, SC 12345 • commun.i.cation@college.edu • (321) 555-6789

EDUCATION
College of Knowledge, Your Town, SC, December 2014
Bachelor of Arts in Communication
Concentration: Corporate and Organizational Communication
Minor: Spanish

Course Highlights: Media Law, Writing for the Mass Media, Marketing, Public Relations, International Business, Communication Research Methods

Study Abroad, University of Madrid, Spring 2013

RELEVANT EXPERIENCE
Caring Ministries, Your Town, SC
PR & Marketing Intern, Fall 2014
- o Assisted in the development of a new ad for the nonprofits annual campaign and largest fundraising event
- o Wrote press releases, participated in campaign planning sessions and media outlet pitches
- o Coordinated campaign outreach events with the communications department

WCTV – ABC News 4NBC Universal, Any Town, SC
Intern, Summer 2013
- o Participated in the development of live broadcasting in the departments of live business news, public relations, and editing
- o Researched, outlined, and analyzed current events in the surrounding counties

Channel Surfer, Inc. – HITS 101 FM, Any Town, GA
Intern, Summer 2012
- o Researched relevant topics and wrote the daily news broadcasts for on-air shows
- o Assisted top DJ's in writing and organizing shows and participated on-air
- o Aided in the interviewing process of celebrity music artists at the annual BEATS Concert 2012

WORK EXPERIENCE
The Peach Club, Any Town, GA
Hostess, Summer 2009-2011
- o Provided excellent customer service in a fast-paced environment
- o Handled all public relations and marketing activities for restaurant's philanthropic efforts

SKILLS
- o Proficient in Microsoft Office Word, PowerPoint, Excel, Access, Photoshop and Second Life
- o Strong written and oral communication skills in English and Spanish

ACTIVITIES
- o The Street Observer, *News Reporter,* 2012-present
- o Student Alumni Association, *Member,* 2012-present
- o Delta Gamma Sorority, *Member,* 2011-present

Action Verbs

Communication
Addressed
Arbitrated
Authored
Corresponded
Directed
Drafted
Edited
Enlisted
Expressed
Formulated
Influenced
Interpreted
Interviewed
Lectured
Mediated
Moderated
Negotiated
Persuaded
Presented
Promoted
Publicized
Reported

Creative
Acted
Arranged
Conceptualized
Created
Designed
Developed
Directed
Engineered
Established
Fashioned
Founded
Illustrated
Integrated
Introduced
Invented
Imagined
Modernized
Originated
Performed
Planned

Management
Administered
Assigned
Attained
Authorized
Chaired
Contracted
Consolidated
Coordinated
Delegated
Developed
Directed
Evaluated
Executed
Improved
Increased
Instituted
Lead
Managed
Met goals
Organized
Oversaw
Planned
Prioritized
Produced
Recommended
Reviewed

Technical
Assembled
Calculated
Catalogued
Computed
Designed
Detected
Devised
Engineered
Fabricated
Integrated
Maintained
Operated
Programmed
Remodeled
Revamped
Solved
Streamlined
Trained
Upgraded
Translated

Financial
Accounted
Administered
Allocated
Analyzed
Appraised
Assessed
Audited
Balanced
Budgeted
Calculated
Computed
Developed
Downsized
Forecasted
Generated
Managed
Marketed
Planned
Projected
Researched
Secured

Office Support
Allocated
Approved
Arranged
Catalogued
Classified
Compiled
Dispatched
Executed
Formulated
Generated
Implemented
Inspected
Monitored
Operated
Organized
Prepared
Processed
Purchased
Recorded
Retrieved
Scheduled
Specified
Systematized
Tabulated
Validated

Helping
Advised
Assisted
Clarified
Coached
Counseled
Developed Rapport
Encouraged
Educated
Empathized
Established
Relationships
Expedited
Facilitated
Familiarized
Guided
Mentored
Referred
Rehabilitated
Represented
Supported
Supplied
Rectified

Teaching
Adapted
Advised
Clarified
Coached
Communicated
Coordinated
Demonstrated
Developed
Educated
Enabled
Encouraged
Evaluated
Explained
Facilitated
Guided
Informed
Initiated
Instructed
Motivated
Persuaded
Presented
Set goals
Stimulated

Writing
Addressed
Authored
Composed
Drafted
Edited
Formulated
Inscribed
Printed
Produced
Publicized
Recorded
Reproduced
Scribed
Scripted
Transcribed
Wrote

Research
Analyzed
Assessed
Collected
Compared
Critiqued
Diagnosed
Documented
Dissected
Evaluated
Examined
Extracted
Hypothesized
Identified
Inspected
Interpreted
Interviewed
Investigated
Located
Measured
Observed
Questioned
Reviewed
Screened
Summarized
Surveyed
Synthesized
Systematized

RESUMÉ DO'S & DON'TS

Do

- o Use a conservative font (Times New Roman, Arial, etc.) between 10-12 point in size. You want to make your resumé easy to read, so keep it simple.
- o Set your margins between 0.5 and 1.0 inches.
- o Keep your resumé up to date (especially your contact information)!
- o If printing your resumé, print it on white or off-white bond/resumé paper (darker colors don't copy well).

Don't

- o Don't use a resumé template! They can be difficult to edit in the future, so save yourself the headache later!
- o Don't include personal information such as age, gender, etc. *(However, if planning to apply to an internship/job in another country, that may need to be included.)*
- o Don't use "I" statements.
- o Don't *exaggerate* or lie on your resumé!

What is a cover letter?

A **cover letter** is an introduction to a potential employer and, like your resumé, is a marketing tool! It is an opportunity for you to tell your story — not just to reiterate what can be viewed on your resumé. Too often, many people will simply restate what is included in their resumé. Instead you should use this opportunity to draw connections between your experience/skills and what the employer is looking for, as well as telling them *why* you are interested in the position.

As with the resumé, cover letters are more effective when they are targeted to a specific job and/or organization. Employers can tell when you have submitted a generic cover letter and are not likely to be impressed. If you don't take time to research the job/company and to consider how your experience/skills relate to their needs, it translates to a lack of genuine interest on your part! Personalize each letter and help them understand why they should consider you as a viable candidate, but keep it simple. One page should be sufficient for you to spark interest!

Additionally, your cover letter expresses a great deal about your writing skills. When you share your resumé with others for proofreading, you'll also want them to review your cover letter to help make sure it's clear, concise, and free of errors.

The following page gives you an outline and a sample of what a cover letter could look like and what you may want to include. Contact your campus career center if you need help getting started and/or advice for writing your best cover letter.

SAMPLE COVER LETTER

66 Any Street
Your Town, SC 25555
March 20, 2015

Ms. Sarah Douglas, Editor
Redbook Magazine
300 W. 57th St.
New York, NY 10019

Dear Ms. Douglas:

I am writing to express my interest in the Assistant to the Features Editor position at *Redbook*. As a Communication major at the College of Knowledge with a minor in Women's and Gender Studies, I would love to be part of a publication that inspires women to love themselves and find happiness in all aspects and stages of their lives.

Through my experience with *Styled!,* a monthly magazine for women in the Any Town area. I have had the opportunity to collaborate on articles ranging from skin cancer prevention and identification to beach picnic ideas. Additionally, working with a staff of eight to build a new campus publication, *George,* was one of the most rewarding and invaluable journalist experiences I have had. In this position, I worked as assigning editor, writer, and copy editor. Nothing was more gratifying than seeing the final product published.

My love for the fashion industry was instrumental in my decision to study abroad in Milan, Italy last fall. Not surprisingly, I found a way to combine my trip with my love for journalism. Eager to let the world know the details of my life-changing adventure, I contributed a weekly feature, "My Bella Life" to our campus magazine, even while I was away from campus.

I am passionate about the magazine industry and the people that inhabit it — both in the publishing industry as well as the readers. I am a mission driven person who wants to make a contribution, and the best way I know how to do this is through working with a magazine where I can contribute my strong communication and research skills.

I look forward to the opportunity for a personal interview in order to discuss my qualifications with you in more detail. Please do not hesitate to contact me with any questions, and thank you for your consideration.

Sincerely,

Abigail Gents

Enclosure

COVER LETTER OUTLINE

Your Street Address
City, State, Zip Code
Date

(Space down four spaces)

Ms. Betty Wilson
Director of Recruiting
Jefferson Industries, Inc.
1234 Broad Parkway
Greenville, SC 29602

Dear Ms. Wilson:

The opening paragraph should state why you are writing and why you are interested in the organization. If you are writing a letter of application, you should name the position for which you are applying and tell the employer how you became aware of the position. A letter of inquiry should provide evidence of your career-mindedness; it helps to refer to specific job functions, if not the job title. If you were referred to the employer by another person, this is the best place to mention that person's name, and point out that he or she suggested you write.

The middle paragraph is where you highlight specific skills you possess that are relevant to the job or employer. This paragraph should strongly outline your strengths for the position and your motives for seeking employment with this organization. Remember to be concise and give specific examples of your skills. If you have qualifications noted on your resumé, this is the opportunity to discuss how they relate to this particular position or employer, but do not just repeat information that is on your resumé.

The closing paragraph states what you will do next (such as calling to arrange an interview at the employer's convenience), or what you would like the recipient of the letter to do next. An assertive statement explaining what you plan to do and what you hope the employer will do is harder to ignore than a vague request for consideration. Also, here is where you thank the employer for considering you for this position.

Sincerely,

(Space down four spaces and sign your name here)

Your Name Typed

Enclosure (This indicates that your resume is enclosed)

If you're having trouble writing about your skills, refer back to the Transferable Skills worksheets. Review the skills you identified and how you gained them. Consider how those skills relate (or transfer) to what is being required for a career or in the industry you're considering. It may even help to talk out your thoughts with others.

SUMMARY

Now that you have spent some time getting familiar with, and working through, the career development process, you should feel more comfortable in setting a few goals toward declaring your major or gaining experience in a career field of interest. You may not have a definitive road map quite yet, but at this point, you should be more aware of your major and/or career options based on interests, values, and skills. With this awareness, you can then more confidently rule out unrealistic or unwanted options and focus your attention on those that hold some real potential. At the very least, you may have confirmed that the path you were considering is the best for you at this time.

So instead of asking yourself, "What do I want to do for the rest of my life?" ask, "What do I want to do next?" From that point, prioritize which major or career path you would like to explore first; then create action steps to gain the knowledge, skills, or experience you need to help make a more confident decision to move toward your future major or career. *And don't forget to stop and ask for directions from advisors and career center professionals along the way!*

Rev Your Engine

Using your campus career center's job board, locate a job or internship posting that you would be interested in applying for (even if you are not planning to apply just yet). Read through the job description and physically highlight (with a marker or using the highlight feature on your computer) keywords and skills that you think may be most important. Next, compare those highlighted words or phrases with your skills on the Transferable Skills worksheet. Where do they match up? Which skills are you lacking that are required for the job/internship? How can you gain those skills?

- o If you have already created a resumé, are those highlighted skills mentioned in your descriptions? If not, where might you be able to add in some of those keywords to create a more targeted resumé?
- o If you're working on your cover letter, use the highlighted keywords to help you shape what you want to write about related to your experience.

CITATIONS _____

Bolles, R.N. (2012). *What Color Is Your Parachute? A Practical Manual for Job-Hunters and Career Changers.* New York, NY: Ten Speed Press.

College of Charleston Career Center (2014). *The Guide for Career Planning.*

Holland, J.L. (1992). *Making Vocational Choices* (2nd ed.). Odessa, FL: Psychological Assessment Resources.

National Association of Colleges and Employers. (2013, October 2). *Job Outlook 2014: The candidate skills/ qualities employers want.* Retrieved from http://www.naceweb.org/s10022013/job-outlook-skills-quality.aspx

United States Department of Labor Bureau of Labor Statistics. (2012, September 18). *Employee Tenure Summary.* Retrieved from http://www.bls.gov/news.release/tenure.nr0.htm

POST TEST/QUIZ

1. What are the 4 components of self-exploration and the 3 components of career exploration?

    Self-Exploration   Career Exploration
    1.   1.
    2.   2.
    3.   3.
    4.

2. What is the difference between choosing a major vs. choosing a career?

    _____

    _____

    _____

3. What is the purpose of an informational interview?

    _____

    _____

    _____

4. Name at least 4 examples of experiential learning.
    1.
    2.
    3.
    4.
    Additional examples?_____

5. What are transferable skills?

    _____

    _____

    _____

6. Which type of resumé is constructed to highlight skills and abilities that tie directly to the position you are seeking?

_____

_____

_____

CHAPTER 8

DESTINATION: HEALTHY SUCCESS

By Michelle Futrell

1. **LEARNING OUTCOMES: QUESTIONS TO NAVIGATE**
   a. What is the difference between health and wellness?
   b. What are the key nutrients and dietary guidelines?
   c. What are the benefits of regular exercise and how much do you need?
   d. Why is water the most essential nutrient and how much should you consume?
   e. What are some common wellness challenges and how can you best manage these?
   f. What strategies can be used to maximize good oxygen uptake?
   g. What is a personal philosophy and why is it important?
   h. What role does rest play to health and wellness?
   i. What are some of the common health-related implications of stress and how can you manage your stress?
   j. What is emotional intelligence?

2. **KEY CONCEPTS**
   a. Health and wellness
   b. Nutrition
   c. Exercise
   d. Water
   e. Control
   f. Oxygen
   g. Unity
   h. Rest
   i. Stress management
   j. Emotional Intelligence

INTRODUCTION

Just as your educational journey is nothing more than a series of choices, your personal health and wellness choices are key factors in the way you will complete your journey. You can change cars, you can change the direction you drive, but you are the only person who should drive your car.

Begin by defining the concepts of **health** and **wellness.** The *American Heritage Dictionary* defines health as "The overall condition of an organism at a given time; soundness, especially of body or mind; freedom from disease; and a condition of optimal well-being." You can see that this definition focuses on the way your body is functioning at a given time, and the absence of any disease state or situation that is detracting from normal function.

Wellness on the other hand, dives deeper into the collaborative relationship among the factors that allow you to function at optimal levels. Wellness is defined as "enjoying health and vigor of mind, body, and spirit" by *Webster's 11th New Collegiate Dictionary*. The combination of physical health, mental health, and emotional/spiritual health is necessary for optimal function and productivity.

In every area of your life, there are things you can alter and things that are outside your scope of control. This is no different in the areas of health and wellness. Some of your health profile is driven by genetics. The good news is that of the conditions that contribute to death, 51% are impacted by lifestyle choices while the remaining 49% are impacted by genetics (19%), healthcare (10%), and environmental exposure (20%).

Why is this good news? It's good news because this means that the choices you make daily can influence whether or not you may face one of these conditions or if you do, these choices can help you manage the impact one of these conditions might have on your life expectancy.

Date _____ Class _____

FAMILY TREE ACTIVITY _____

Close your eyes and picture a giant oak tree. The tree has deep roots and many soaring branches filled with leaves and luscious fruits and vegetables. What kinds of fruits and vegetables do you see? Do you see apples, watermelons, and pumpkins? Do you see bananas, asparagus, and green beans? Do you see rich colors and fully ripe fruit or do you see splotches on the skin or withering, unappetizing fruit?

Now think about your family members and what you know of their health history. Do you have relatives that are overweight, obese, underweight, or at a normal healthy weight? Do you have relatives with chronic medical conditions like heart disease, stroke, high blood pressure, diabetes, or mental health disorders? These are all factors that are impacted by your genetic profile. You cannot change your genes, but you can manage the genes you have been given. It is important that you know the medical conditions that run in your family so that you can make appropriate lifestyle choices to minimize the impact of these genetic factors.

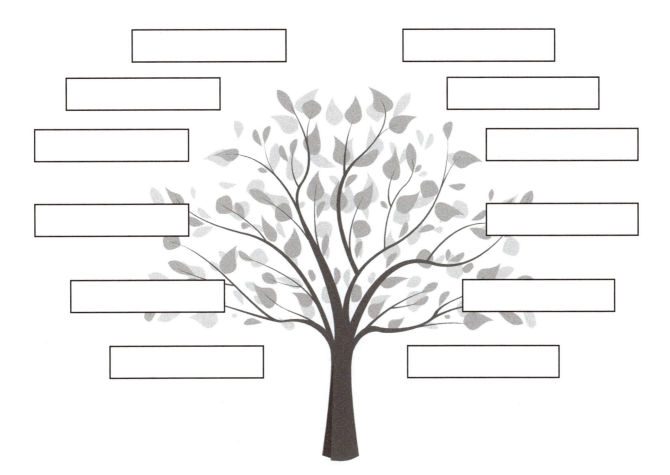

In the each of the boxes on your family tree, identify your relatives from your grandparents, through your parents, aunts, and uncles, down through you and your siblings. For each person you have identified, list any chronic medical conditions that person has managed. If anyone has already passed away, indicate their cause of death. You may have to consult with your relatives in order to completely fill in the table. When you have completed the chart, answer the questions provided.

1. Name the top five medical conditions identified by your research. _____

_____

_____

_____

_____

2. Which of those conditions have genetic connections? _____

_____

_____

_____

_____

3. What steps might you need to take to reduce the impact these genetic conditions might have on your health and wellness?

_____

_____

_____

_____

_____

_____

_____

_____

It is just as important to set goals in the areas of health and wellness as it is in other areas of your life. Remember when setting goals, it is often helpful to structure them using a SMART goal format.

WHAT IS A SMART GOAL?

A SMART goal has the following characteristics:

      S: Specific (Who, What, Where, When, Why)

      M: Measureable (Concrete criteria for determining that the goal has been met)

      A: Attainable (Aligns with your values, attitudes, abilities, and skills)

      R: Realistic (A level at which you are willing and able to work)

      T: Time Frame (Specific period of time at which you will re-evaluate and refine your goal)

Poorly written goal: I want to get in shape.

Well-written goal: In 3 months, I will improve my cardiovascular fitness by being able to jog for 20 minutes without stopping.

In the areas of health and wellness, most goals center around changing a behavior or a habit. In order to change a habit, you have to create a new habit. According to the work on habit forming by Lally (2010), it takes on average 66 days to make a new behavior automatic. If you have selected a particularly difficult habit to change, you may need to break the new behavior down into smaller more manageable pieces. Implement each piece one at a time and commit to the new habit for two months. The research also suggests that missing one day of your new habit will not significantly impact your ability to create the new habit. So don't get down on yourself. Remember, you aren't perfect. At the end of 60 days, you can implement your next baby step.

Suppose your goal is to lose your "freshman 15." In order to lose 15 pounds, you know that you must burn more calories than you take in each day. To alter your energy balance, you can limit the calories you take in or increase the calories you expend. In the first month you choose to decrease your consumption of soda from four sodas a day to two, resulting in a 300-calorie deficit each day. After a month when this has become a habit, you decide to add exercise to your routine. You set a goal to walk for 30 minutes at least 5 days a week. Your new exercise plan creates a 750-calorie per week deficit. At the end of two months, simply implementing these two small "baby step" goals, you will have created an 11,000+ calorie deficit that is equivalent to approximately 3.25 pounds.

Checkpoint

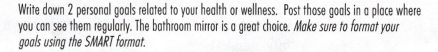

Write down 2 personal goals related to your health or wellness. Post those goals in a place where you can see them regularly. The bathroom mirror is a great choice. *Make sure to format your goals using the SMART format.*

1. _____

_____

2. _____

_____

Health and wellness concerns often take a back seat when you are faced with the various stresses that life throws at you. It is challenging to eat well when you are trying to work 30 hours a week, take a full course load, and manage a difficult roommate. It is hard to find time for personal reflection and meditation when you are only getting four hours of sleep each night and your parents are going through a divorce. It is difficult to say "no" to friends who want to go out and party on a Thursday night when you haven't spent time with them in weeks due to work and personal issues.

Just as you must set academic priorities, you must be conscious of making positive health and wellness choices as well. The acronym NEWCOURSE gives us a positive way to look at the various components of a healthy lifestyle.

NEWCOURSE
N: Nutrition
E: Exercise
W: Water
C: Control
O: Oxygen
U: Unity
R: Rest
S: Stress Management
E: Emotional Health

"If we could give every individual the right amount of nourishment and exercise, not too little and not too much, we would have found the safest way to health." ~ Hippocrates

As you read, evaluate your own personal habits for each of these components and identify areas that you may wish to address.

N: Nutrition

Nutrition is nothing more than a series of daily choices. You choose everything that you put into your body in the form of food or drink. In reality, there are no "good" foods and no "bad" foods. Food is ESSENTIAL. The word **essential,** when referring to nutrition, means something different than it does in any other context. In regard to nutrition, essential means that the nutrient must be consumed in your diet because the body is unable to manufacture the substance. For example, vitamin C is an essential nutrient and must be consumed in the foods that you eat, but cholesterol is not essential and your body can manufacture as much as it needs from the other foods you consume.

You must eat in order to sustain life. All foods can fit into a healthful diet, as long as nutrient needs are being met at caloric levels that allow you to maintain a healthy body weight.

There are three keys to healthy diet:

1. Adequacy: consumption of adequate nutrients to maintain body systems and support a healthy weight.
2. Balance: foods types and amounts are balanced across the various food groups.
3. Variety: a variety of choices are made within each of the nutrient categories to allow consumption of required nutrients and other substances like phytochemicals and antioxidants.

There are six Essential Nutrient categories. Consumption of each of these essential nutrients is required to sustain health, but within each category some choices are healthier than others.

1. **CARBOHYDRATES** are the substances in food that are composed of varying numbers and structures of sugar molecules. The primary purpose of carbohydrates is to provide the body with energy. Carbohydrates range from simple sugars like glucose (blood sugar), sucrose (table sugar), and lactose (milk sugar) to more complex carbohydrates. Complex carbohydrates are also known as starches and dietary fiber. When you are making healthy selections in the carbohydrate category, focus on the following:
    o   Select whole grains (>3g fiber/serving)
    o   Eat fruits and vegetables (5 servings/day of any combination)
    o   Leave skins on fruits and vegetables whenever possible
    o   Avoid juices
    o   Skip refined white flour and processed food choices

Scenic Overlook

Is sugar good for your brain? Sugar or blood glucose is the only energy source that you can utilize to support brain function. When blood sugar levels drop, you may feel sluggish, foggy, or have difficulty processing information or making decisions. This is particularly important if you are walking into a test, as you need your brain to be functioning at its highest level. Eating a meal that contains some carbohydrates 3-4 hours prior to a key exam, then consuming a beverage with some sugar 10-15 minutes prior to walking in to the classroom may improve your brain's ability to work at the highest level. Why do you think your elementary school teacher used to pass out hard candy for you to suck on during standardized tests? Remember, artificial sweeteners, like aspartame in a diet soda, do not contain sugar and therefore have no impact on blood sugar.

Imagine you have a big math test on Friday at noon. When and what might you choose to eat to maximize your brain power for the test?

2. **PROTEINS** are primarily used for growth and repair of body tissues but they also serve as a secondary energy source. The building blocks of all proteins are amino acids. There are 20 amino acids. Nine of those are essential and must be consumed in our diet. A food that contains all nine essential amino acids is said to be a complete protein. Complete proteins are found primarily in animal sources although a select few plant sources, like quinoa and soy, also contain all 9 essential amino acids. When you think about adding protein to your diet, meat products probably come to mind. Low fat, lean cuts of meat like fish and chicken are good protein options but you should also consider the following plant options:
   o   Grains: barley, cornmeal, oats, rice, tortillas, whole-grain breads, enriched pasta
   o   Legumes: dried beans, lentils, dried peas, peanuts, soy
   o   Seeds and Nuts: sesame seeds, sunflower seeds, walnuts, cashews
   o   Veggies: leafy greens, broccoli

3. **FATS** are composed of fatty acids and triglycerides and can be broken down into several categories:
   o   Saturated fats are found primarily in animal products, such as meat, butter, and cheese, and in palm and coconut oils. You should attempt to limit your saturated fat consumption as diets high in saturated fat can increase the risk of developing heart disease.
   o   Unsaturated fats are found primarily in plant products such as vegetable oils, nuts, seeds, and in fish. Unsaturated fats should be maximized and have been shown to lower blood cholesterol levels.
      –   Omega-3 and Omega-6 Fatty Acids: These essential unsaturated fatty acids are required in the diet and have extremely positive correlations with decreased risk of heart disease and Alzheimer's disease. These fatty acids are found in a limited number of foods like cold water fish (salmon, cod, sardines), walnuts, and flaxseed.
   o   Trans fats are unsaturated fats that are modified to take on the properties of saturated fats. Trans fats are present in hydrogenated oil, margarine, shortening, pastries, and some cooking oils. Trans fats are associated with increased risk of heart disease and you should limit consumption of these fats whenever possible.

Of the three energy bearing nutrients, fat is the most energy dense, meaning it provides more energy per gram than either carbohydrates or fats. However, the energy contained in fat is not as easily accessible as the energy in carbohydrates. In addition to serving as an energy source, fat also provides a means of transporting some vitamins.

4 & 5. VITAMINS and MINERALS are nutrients that perform very specific functions in the body. To promote normal body function, 13 different vitamins and 15 different minerals are required.

Scenic Overlook

Should you take a vitamin or mineral supplement? If you consume a well-balanced diet and make selections from a wide variety of different food choices, then you probably do not need to take a vitamin or mineral supplement. However, if you are like most college students who choose foods based on affordability and availability or if you know your diet is limited in fruits, vegetables, and/ or dairy products, then you may benefit from a generic multi-vitamin and mineral supplement. Do you need to take a multi-vitamin/mineral supplement?

If you choose to take a supplement, the best time to take it to maximize absorption is right before bed.

6. **WATER** is the last of the essential nutrients. You can live much longer without food than you can without water. Water is essential for almost all bodily functions. Most adults need 8-11 cups of water each day from the food and fluids they consume.

There are several other key components in food that promote overall health and well-being.

PHYTOCHEMICALS are chemical substances found in plants that enable the plant to grow and protect themselves against infection and disease. These phytochemicals that give plants their color and flavor serve similar functions when you eat them. Diets rich in phytochemicals have been shown to reduce the risk of some cancers, heart disease, and infection. Some phytochemicals are also antioxidants. **ANTIOXIDANTS** are chemical substances that prevent or repair cell damage that is caused by oxidizing agents such as environmental pollutants, smoke, ozone, and oxygen. Eating a diet rich in brightly-colored fruits and vegetables will provide you with these health-promoting substances.

Dietary Recommendations: Understanding how to make good choices in each of the essential nutrient categories is important, but you may be asking yourself, *"How much of each of those nutrients do I need to be healthy?"* One excellent source of information is www. ChooseMyPlate.gov. This comprehensive website, sponsored by the United States Department of Agriculture (USDA) provides consumers with the most current federal guidelines regarding dietary choices. In addition to nutrition policies and recommendations, that site provides educational materials, recipes, and an interactive nutrition tracking and analysis program.

For the energy bearing nutrients, recommendations are made for the percentage of daily calories that should be consumed in each area.

Nutrient Source	Recommended % of Total Calories
Carbohydrates	45-65%
Proteins	10-15%
Fats	<25-30%

For the other nutrients, a Dietary Reference Intake (DRI) is provided. The DRI provides the recommended intake levels that meet the nutritional needs of 97% of the healthy population. The DRIs are designed to promote health and reduce the risk of chronic disease. In order to make recommendations readily available to the public, a Nutrition Facts Panel is also required on the label of all foods composed of more than one ingredient. The information contained on this panel is standardized to allow the public to easily compare one product to another.

Key parts of the Nutrition Label:

Serving Size: The amount of the product considered to be one serving. The information on the label is found in one serving of the product. *Beware: Not all serving sizes are standard, even across comparable products.*

Calories: The total energy created when one serving of the product is digested.

% Daily Value: This indicates the percent of the agreed upon standard of daily intake obtained from one serving of the food product. This is based on a 2,000-calorie diet of 60% carbohydrates, 30% fat, and 10% protein. *Note: If you consume more or less than 2,000 calories a day, the percentages would need to be adjusted.*

Nutrient Amounts: Only the total amount of each of the energy-bearing nutrients (carbohydrates, proteins, and fats and their breakdowns), Cholesterol, and Sodium must be included on the label.

Other Vitamins and Minerals: Vitamins A and C and the minerals Calcium and Iron are included as % Daily Values.

Nutrition Facts	
Serving Size 1/4 Cup (30g)	
Servings Per Container About 38	
Amount Per Serving	
Calories 200 Calories from Fat 150	
	% Daily Value*
Total Fat 17g	**26%**
Saturated Fat 2.5g	**13%**
Trans Fat 0g	
Cholesterol 0mg	**0%**
Sodium 120mg	**5%**
Total Carbohydrate 7g	**2%**
Dietary Fiber 2g	**8%**
Sugars 1g	
Protein 5g	
Vitamin A 0% • Vitamin C 0%	
Calcium 4% • Iron 8%	
*Percent Daily Values are based on a 2,000 calorie diet.	

It may seem that meeting all of these recommendations each day is impossible. If the truth were told, it is virtually impossible to eat a perfect diet every day. The good news is you don't have to consume a perfect diet every day. Your body has adaptive mechanisms in place that allow you to conserve and store nutrients when the supply is low and eliminate excessive nutrients so you don't reach a toxic state.

E: Exercise

Exercise is another key component of a healthy lifestyle. The long-term health benefits associated with physical activity are extensive. Unfortunately, 81.6% of adults and 81.8% of adolescents do not get the recommended amount of physical activity. In addition to reducing the risk of many chronic diseases, other benefits of participating in regular physical activity include:
- o   Increased life expectancy
- o   Improved self-image
- o   Improved sleep patterns
- o   Stronger muscles and bones

- o Maintenance of a healthy weight
- o Opportunities for interactions with other people
- o Improved mental health
- o Decreased stress levels
- o Improved flexibility and ease of movement
- o Enhanced brain activity

The Physical Activity Guidelines for adults recommends that inactivity be avoided whenever possible as health benefits are associated with participation in any type of physical activity. Increased health benefits are associated with 150 minutes of moderate intensity or 75 minutes of vigorous intensity aerobic activity each week. Additional health benefits are associated with 300 minutes of moderate intensity or 150 minutes of vigorous intensity aerobic exercise each week. In addition to aerobic activity, muscular strengthening exercises that incorporate all major muscle groups should occur two or more days a week.

Since any type of activity produces health benefits, the type of exercise you choose is less important than the fact that you are up and moving. You should choose activities that you enjoy, as you are more likely to continue to participate if you are having fun. Varying your exercise routine will decrease the chance of boredom, and finding a friend to exercise with also improves compliance. There are many excellent computer and mobile applications that make it easy to track your activity levels and many applications also include the option of monitoring nutrition at the same time.

In addition to the health-related benefits associated with exercise, it is important to note that exercise also enhances brain activity. Several research studies have shown that resistance and aerobic training improve memory. Most recently, studies have indicated that aerobic training increases the size of the hippocampus, which is the brain center responsible for memory and learning. We also know that exercise reduces stress and anxiety, which are also known to decrease cognition. So start exercising!

W: Water

Of the 6 essential nutrients, **water** is often categorized as the most essential. You can live a lot longer without food than you can without water. In fact, water makes up almost 70% of your total body weight. Adequate amounts of water are required to support a variety of important bodily functions like maintaining blood volume, regulating body temperature, aiding in digestion and excretion, and carrying oxygen and nutrients.

Unlike other nutrients, the body cannot readily store water and therefore you must consume adequate fresh water to support bodily processes every day. In fact, most adults lose 2.5-3 L of water every day and those losses are increased in hot weather and during exercise. A loss of even 2% body weight can result in dehydration. Dehydration can result in headaches, tiredness, mood changes, slowed responses, and confusion.

So how much water should you be consuming every day? The baseline recommendation is 8-10 cups a day with women typically requiring slightly less than males. The easiest way to tell if you are properly hydrated is to monitor the color of your urine. If you are well hydrated, your urine should be a pale yellow (the color of weak lemonade). A good rule of thumb is to try to never feel thirsty. The thirst mechanism is triggered when your body begins to become dehydrated so if you are thirsty, you are already water depleted.

TIPS FOR CONSUMING ENOUGH WATER:

- Take a drink at every water fountain you see
- Carry a refillable bottle of water with you
- If you don't like the taste of water, try some creative infusions like lemon, cucumber, raspberries, or cilantro
- Water-based beverages like tea or powdered drink mixes do count
- Drink before and after exercise
- Drink two glasses of water when you wake up
- Drink a glass of water 30 minutes before every meal

C: Control

You are constantly bombarded with distractions that try to pull you away from your priorities. Many of these distractions come disguised as fun, social activities. No one is arguing that you shouldn't have fun. Everyone needs a little fun in their lives. Fun provides you the opportunity to unwind, moderate stress levels, and connect with other people. However, fun can become detrimental to your health when you fail to control the choices you make. It is important that you are able to find a balance between the choices you need to make to meet your goals and the myriad of things that might be distracting you.

You can control your distractions by first identifying them. Make a list of the things that most commonly distract you and eat up a lot of unnecessary time. You might choose to include things like relationships, television, alcohol, video games, social media, substance misuse, greek life, or extracurricular activities just to name a few. If you have been completely honest with yourself, you can probably identify a few of the distractions that you can control to create more balance in your life. Start slowly. Choose one distraction and see if you can identify a specific action step that you will try for the next month. When you have that distraction under control, move to something else on your list.

Here's an example: Sarah is a junior who really wants to go to nursing school when she graduates. She knows that well-rounded students with good leadership skills are considered more favorably by graduate school admissions committees. With that in mind, she is vice president of her sorority, a member of the pre-nursing club, a volunteer at the local children's hospital two days a week, and has just joined the club crew team. Sarah is extremely social and often joins her friends to go out at some of the local establishments at least 3 nights a week to unwind from the stress of school. Sarah is appalled to find that at mid-term all of her grades are below a C. This is a wake-up call to Sarah, as she understands that her grades are equally important to her future. Sarah sits down and maps all her activities out on a weekly calendar and realizes that she is not leaving herself enough study time. Sarah decides to cut back her volunteer hours at the hospital to one day each week and remove herself from the crew team. She also decides to tell her friends that she is only going to go out on the weekends, not on school nights so she can find more time to focus on her studies. Sarah's choices pay off. When final grades come out, she has raised her grades in all of her classes to a B or better.

The message here is you can have fun and still meet your goals if you can find balance and master the concept of everything in moderation.

BALANCE AND MODERATION: KEYS TO A SUCCESSFUL TRIP

By Kate Tiller

If you were on a road trip, you would not drive 100 miles per hour, but you probably would not drive 20 miles per hour under the speed limit either. You would not schedule a rest stop every 30 minutes, but you probably would not drive for hours without taking one. Learning to find balance and the art of moderation will help you manage your road to academic recovery.

Often you hear college students joke that they can only pick two among the following: academics, social life, and sleep. Though they are joking, they are right that finding the balance between academics and your social life, not to mention other responsibilities that you might have, is difficult. Finding balance means that you do have a social life, that you are committed to your academic success, and that you can also be responsible for other parts of your life. In the chapter on time management, you learned some time management tools, and in the chapter called "Checking Your Mirrors," you had the opportunity to think about the values that are important to you. Balance is taking your values and finding the ability to manage your time so that you have a life where you can live your values.

Additionally, when you think about the social scene at your school, you may think about clubs and organizations or friends that are really positive in your life. You might not spend a lot of time partying. But, maybe for you, the social scene is the party scene. Just remember that moderation in all things gives you the opportunity to benefit from the many opportunities that lie before you.

Because of your academic situation, you may feel like you suddenly need to spend every single minute of your time on school. This will not work! Instead, it will likely lead to feelings of stress and a potential to feel very overwhelmed. Again, throughout this text, you have had the opportunity to learn new skills that will help you commit to effectively using the time you spend on your academics.

What is important about balance and moderation is knowing that the right fit will not look the same for everyone or even the same for you at different points in your life. You may need to spend more time on your academics during this semester than your roommate does. You may need more time with your friends, or you may find that you crave a little more alone time. Just remember, your college journey is not one you make alone. If you feel you are getting sidetracked, there are plenty of services on your campus to get you back on the road to success.

Checkpoint

Take a moment to reflect upon the different distractions that you face on a regular basis. These can be both positive and negative distractions. Then identify two distractions that you can modify or control to become more healthy or productive.

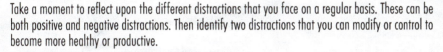

1. _____

2. _____

O: Oxygen

Oxygen is essential for all body cells to function. Your body's primary system for producing the energy you need to sustain activities of low intensity and long duration, like all the activities you do every day, relies on oxygen. While oxygen is vital, where you get this oxygen is also important for overall good health. You probably spend the majority of your time indoors, whether that is in class, at work, or at home. Contaminants in the air inside buildings can often be up to five times higher than in outside air. The small exception may be urban areas with high levels of air pollution, especially at high traffic times of the day. Spending the majority of your time breathing air with even minor contaminants can result in headaches, irritation of the throat or eyes, and sinus problems. How can you ensure that you are maximizing a good supply of oxygen to your cells? Spend some time outside every day. Exposure to sunlight for as little as 15 minutes three times a week will allow your body to produce enough vitamin D to meet the recommendations for this vitamin. Exercising regularly will teach your body how to take in and use oxygen effectively. You could also participate in deep breathing exercises to maximize oxygen exchange. You might even choose to bring the outside in by putting a green plant in every room. Plants have been shown to significantly reduce typical household pollution in a 24-hour period.

U: Unity

Unity refers to the collaboration of mind, body, and spirit. In order to be your best self, each of these components must be in harmony with one another. When your mental or emotional health, physical health, and spiritual health are all working together, you will find that you are much more productive and fulfilled in the things you are doing. It is important that you have a clear understanding of yourself and the things that you believe and value. This will allow you to develop a more unified sense of purpose. You should consider spending some time thinking about and defining your own personal philosophy.

GET INVOLVED; MAKE CONNECTIONS!

By Kate Tiller

Taking care of your physical and mental health will play a major role in getting you back on the right track academically. Getting involved and connected on your campus can contribute to better overall well-being. Whether it is using the services your campus offers — like counseling or residence life — or getting involved with student life activities, finding a place where you can express yourself will help you feel like you are not on this journey alone!

While every campus is different, most campuses offer some sort of counseling services. You may have specific mental health concerns or you may be dealing with stress or a difficult life situation and feel like you need to talk to somebody other than just a friend or family member. Counseling services departments offer the opportunity to speak with someone who is trained to help you work through your feelings and find a path to healthier living. If you ever feel like you are going to hurt yourself, or perhaps if you are concerned about someone else hurting himself, you should reach out to this department or your campus police immediately.

Even if you do not feel like you need counseling services, getting involved is for everybody! If you live on campus, one of the first ways to get involved is through your residence hall staff. Often they have programming right where you live to help you meet other people. Your resident assistant (RA) can also be a key person with ideas to help you make connections on campus.

Whether you live on or off campus, you might find your place with your campus's recreation services, student life, or other student organizations. Many campuses offer intramural sports, organized physical activities or classes, and a gym. All of these are great ways to meet people while taking good care of yourself.

Your campus likely has some sort of student life programming each semester and offers student clubs and organizations. Sometimes it can be nerve-wracking to take the first step to go to these meetings, but think about it, the other people who are showing up for these meetings are interested in the same thing you are! You already have something to talk about. These groups can range from Greek-letter organizations or faith-based groups to clubs of people who are interested in politics, history, or community service. That just covers a few of the many types of groups that are available on many campuses.

No matter what outlet you find, finding that place where you can connect with people will make you feel like you belong on your campus. Research shows that engaged students are more likely to be successful students!

What is a personal philosophy and why do you need one? Webster's Dictionary defines philosophy as the study of the ideas related of knowledge, truth, love, and the meaning of life. You can think of it more personally as exploring what you know, how you know it, and why it is important that you know it. It is important that you develop your own personal philosophy because understanding who you are and what you know and value can help provide direction as you make decisions regarding your personal development. In addition, it will improve your overall effectiveness and influence your behavior. Decisions you make that align with your personal philosophy tend to be the most productive and fulfilling, as they help you work toward meeting your goals.

ACTIVITY: DEVELOPING YOUR OWN PERSONAL PROFESSIONAL PHILOSOPHY _ _ _ _ _ _ _ _ _ _ _ _ _ _

Julie is majoring in education. For one of her classes, she has been asked to reflect and then write her own personal professional philosophy. This is what Julie wrote:

*My life can best be summarized by the phrase **Never Stop Learning**. I don't ever want to be content to do things just because that is the way it has always been done. I want to constantly question, continually read, and consistently grow and evolve as a person and a teacher.*

I believe that I must model my philosophies daily, and eventually model them to the students I will teach.

I believe preparation is vital. I will get to class on time and prepared to learn. I will do my homework and reading outside of class so that I am prepared to learn. Preparation also involves removing all the other distractions and focusing just on that class for the 50 or 75 minutes allotted.

I believe that everyone has the capacity to learn. I believe in one way or another everyone is a teacher. Each person has gifts and expertise they can share and they must feel free to express their thoughts and ideas in an open environment.

I believe as the saying goes "everything you need to know you learned in kindergarten." Respect others and you will gain their respect in return. People are more open to others who seem approachable. Taking the time to learn people's names makes them feel valued and appreciated.

I believe that excitement and a positive attitude is contagious. If I am excited about learning then others around me will share that excitement. Above all, if learning is fun then we will Never Stop Learning!

Before you begin writing your personal philosophy, answer the following questions:
What do you deem important?

What do you value?

What do you believe?

Why do you believe it?

Now you are ready to write. As you write, you may want to consider including some of the following in your personal, professional philosophy:
o Discuss your personal values (i.e., qualities or characteristics that describe who you are, what you believe in, and what you do).
o Explain a specific example of how your values have resulted in principle-based decisions that are reflective of your personal philosophy of life.
o Describe your professional goals and aspirations.
o Identify a current activity that illustrates how you are working toward the accomplishment of your goals in a way that is congruent with your values.
o Give an illustration of how your values will interface with the type of professional actions you believe are important in your chosen career.

R: Rest

Good quality **rest** is usually difficult to find on a college campus. College students are pulled in a multitude of different directions by various responsibilities and distractions. The mere challenge of living in a dorm or apartment with several other students is far from the ideal environment for deep, restful sleep. Sleep, however, plays a key role in overall health and well-being.

Most people need between 6-10 hours of sleep per night. The average recommendation is 8 hours. The goal is to wake up feeling refreshed and maintain focus throughout the day without feeling overly tired. You should not have to rely on stimulants or "pick me ups" like caffeine to help you wake up or keep you awake.

During the sleep process your body may appear totally at rest, but sleep is actually a very active state in which your body rests and restores its energy. Your brain is busy as well. While you are sleeping, your brain processes the information you have taken in throughout the day. As the sleeping brain processes information, it is able to convert information to long-term memory and sift through irrelevant information so that you only retain the key facts. Some research also shows that as the brain analyzes information from the day, new and different connections and relationships may be established allowing you to solve problems that you may have been working on when you were awake. In fact, these positive influences on memory are only seen during sleep. They do not occur in the same way when you are awake. The lesson to take away from this is: No All-Nighters! Study well and then sleep and let your brain finish the study process for you while you sleep.

TIPS TO IMPROVE YOUR SLEEP HABITS:

- Create a daily routine: Go to bed at the same time. Get up at the same time and exercise at the same time each day.
- During the daytime hours, stay in well lit areas.
- Keep your bedroom dark and quiet.
- Turn off television and music before going to sleep.
- Eat at least four hours before bedtime.
- Turn off all electronic devices (iPad, computer, social media) at least an hour before bedtime.
- Avoid consuming caffeine after dinner.

S: Stress Management

College can be a very exciting time, but it also presents you a variety of challenges as well. These challenges might include large amounts of unstructured free time, new environment, new people, peer pressures, value conflicts, increased personal responsibility, difficult academic coursework, exposure to new experiences, or financial pressures. Any of these factors could be considered a stressor.

The definition of the word **stress** as we use it today, is attributed to Hans Selye, who in 1936 defined stress as "the non-specific response of the body to any demand for change." Stress quickly acquired a negative connotation leading to our more current definition of stress as distress being "physical, mental or emotional strain or tension." This prompted Selye to add the word *eustress,* or positive stress, which occurs when the stressor motivates and improves performance. Examples of eustress might include the pressure to earn a starting position on a team, working hard to get off academic probation, or planning a wedding.

As indicated on The Human Function Curve (Fig. 1), stress can be positive and increase performance until "the hump" or the overload point is reached, at which point performance and health can begin to suffer. Stress that is not kept in check may result in burn-out.

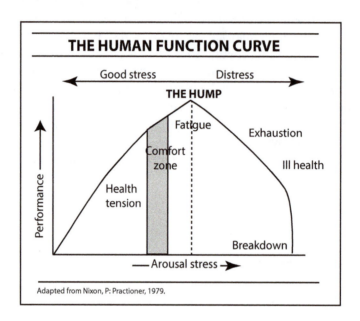

Each person responds to stress differently. Some common symptoms of stress include:

o   Headaches
o   Light headedness, faintness, dizziness
o   Frequent colds, infections, cold sores
o   Heartburn, stomach pain, nausea
o   Chest pain, palpitations, rapid pulse
o   Excess anxiety, worry, guilt, nervousness
o   Anger, frustration, hostility
o   Increased or decreased appetite
o   Insomnia, nightmares, bad dreams
o   Difficulty concentrating
o   Feeling overloaded or overwhelmed
o   Fatigue, weakness

In extreme situations, stress can result in:

o   Depression
o   Anxiety
o   Eating Disorders
o   Substance Abuse

Among college students, alcohol is often used as a means of coping with stress. In fact, stress has been linked to the development of problem drinking behaviors and the inability to cease these behaviors after graduation.

It's important for you to identify the things that make you feel stress. You should also be able to recognize how you respond physically, emotionally, and mentally to stress so that you can take steps to manage or alleviate your stress before you reach the overload point.

The Centers for Disease Control recommends several key ways to manage stress:

o   Avoid drugs and alcohol: While these substances may seem to dull stress feelings, substance abuse can actually exacerbate rather than alleviate the problems associated with stress.

o   Find support: You may find that just sharing the situations you are trying to manage with an unbiased ear can really help you cope with the stress you are feeling. You can turn to a family member, friend, or minister. Most colleges have a counseling center that is also available to provide assistance to students coping with various stressors.

o   Connect socially: A common coping reaction to a stressful situation is to withdraw. Instead, you should focus on reaching out to friends or participating in club or extracurricular activities that allow you to create positive relationships.

o   Take care of yourself: Routinely practicing all of the components we have discussed in this chapter will also help you manage your stress. When you are feeling stressed, it is even more important that you try to eat a healthy, well-balanced diet, exercise, get plenty of sleep, and maintain a normal daily routine. You might also find it helpful to practice relaxation techniques, guided imagery, or deep, abdominal breathing.

o   Stay active: Keeping yourself busy will allow you to focus your energy on other things besides your stressors. You might even choose to participate in some type of volunteer work or community service activity.

It is important to note that there is a key difference between anxiety and stress. As defined by Hans Selye, stress is a response that is caused by some type of stressor. Anxiety is a manifestation of stress that continues after the stressor is gone. In addition, anxiety is often accompanied by feelings of fear or apprehension and often by feelings of impending doom. If you experience symptoms that are more consistent with anxiety than stress, you should share your feelings with a healthcare provider or reach out to the professionals at your campus counseling center.

Some students will experience stress-like symptoms that are caused by a lack of stress. This is called rust-out. Rust-out occurs when you find life and your classes to be dull and not interesting or engaging. You may find yourself feeling very apathetic and unmotivated. This apathy might be directed toward classes, your job, or even social situations. If you are experiencing stress or burn-out symptoms but are not under a lot of stress, you could benefit from a conversation with someone in your counseling center and/or career center who could help you identify your strengths and passions and direct your efforts in those areas.

E: Emotional Health

There is a strong connection between success and the ability to understand and handle your emotions. Just as you must be committed and work hard to maintain and improve your physical health, you must also cultivate your emotional health as well. **Emotional health** refers to your overall psychological well-being. It does not refer to the absence of mental health problems, but instead focuses on your ability to understand your emotions, manage your emotions, perceive the emotions of others, and use those emotions in a positive way. The concept is known as emotional intelligence and has been shown to correlate highly with success. In fact, many companies are now using assessments of emotional intelligence in their hiring process.

The concept of emotional intelligence can be broken down into five elements:

- **Self-Awareness** – Self-awareness refers to the ability to honestly evaluate your own emotions and identify personal strengths and weaknesses. Being aware of your emotions allows you to trust what you are feeling, and can keep your emotions from getting out of control.
- **Self-Regulation** – Self-regulation centers on your ability to control your emotions and redirect disruptive impulses and moods. As you develop your ability to self-regulate, you will become better at making decisions and thinking before acting.
- **Motivation** – Motivation focuses on your ability to work toward end results that you value. You will find yourself drawn toward goals of importance to you and are not solely linked to money or status.
- **Empathy** – Empathy focuses on the ability to recognize what others are feeling and relate to others in a non-judgmental way.
- **Social Skills** – Social skills are best manifested while working with others. Communicating with others, establishing relationships, and managing conflicts are among your strengths if you excel in this element.

The good news is that emotional intelligence can be developed with a little recognition and practice. If you are willing to be completely honest, and can identify areas in which you are currently not as in touch with your emotions or the emotions of others, you can begin to develop your skills in those areas.

Ask yourself these types of questions:

- Do I put myself in someone else's shoes to try to understand what they are feeling?
- Do I rush to make a judgment or do I consider the situation from different viewpoints?
- Am I a hot reactor in a stressful situation or do I take things as they come and manage them?
- Do I work hard because I see value in what I am doing?
- Am I quick to blame others rather than accept personal responsibility for my circumstances?
- Am I humble? Do I seek to be in the spotlight or allow the light to shine on others?
- Do I take into consideration how my actions will make other people feel?
- Do I seek to diffuse conflict when it arises?

SUMMARY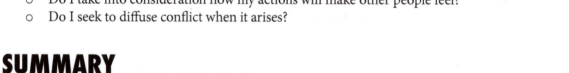

Throughout this chapter you have been asked to evaluate various areas that relate to your personal health and wellness. Each of these components will impact your ability to be successful in the other academic, social, and professional areas of your life. It's not too late to set a NEWCOURSE toward your ultimate destination — Healthy Success.

Rev Your Engine

Complete your own nutrition and exercise analysis. Using the Supertracker feature created by the USDA, create a personal profile and track your food and activity for 7-10 days. This will give you a much better idea of whether or not you are meeting the recommendations for nutrition and exercise. If you're not, then set a goal and begin addressing some of your deficiencies. *Note: There are also many mobile applications that will provide similar tracking information.*

Compare the Nutrition Facts Panel for two comparable products. After reviewing the labels, make a case for the product that you believe is the healthier choice.

Create a plan for improving your EQ (Emotional Intelligence Quotient). If you didn't do it at the earlier checkpoint, use the Internet to identify a free Emotional Intelligence quiz. Use the results of that quiz to identify the areas of emotional intelligence that you can develop more fully. Write 1-2 concrete action steps you will use to develop your emotional intelligence in each area.

REFERENCES

Brown, J.E. (2011). *Nutrition Now (6th Ed.)* Belmont, CA: Thomson Wadsworth.

Casa, D.J., Armstrong, L.E., Hillman, S.K., Montain, S.J., Reiff, R.V., Rich, B.S.E., Roberts, W.O., & Stone, J.A. (2000). National Athletic Trainers Association Position Statement: Fluid Replacement for Athletes. *JAT, 35*(2), 212-224.

Centers for Disease Control and Prevention (2012). *Managing Stress.* Atlanta, GA. Retrieved from www.cdc.gov/features/handlingstress

Emotional Intelligence. (2015). Retrieved from www.danielgoleman.info/topics/emotional-intelligence/

Lally, P., van Jaarsveld, C.H.M., Potts, H.W.W., & Wardle, J. (2010). How are habits formed: Modelling habit formation in the real world. *Eur. J. Soc. Psychol., 40*(6), 998–1009. doi: 10.1002/ejsp.674

Liu, R.H. (2003). Health benefits of fruit and vegetables are from additive and synergistic combinations of phytochemicals. *Am J Clin Nutr*, 78, 5178-5205.

Park et al. (2004). The daily stress and coping process and alcohol use among college students. *Journal of Studies on Alcohol, 65*(1).

Stickgold, R., Ellenbogen, J.M. (2008). Quiet, sleeping brain at work. *Scientific American Mind.*

Ten Brinke, L.F., Bolandzadeh, N., Nagamatsu, L.S., Hsu, C.L., Davis, J.C., Miran-Khan, K., & Liu-Ambrose, T. (2014). Aerobic exercise increases hippocampal volume in older women with probably mild cognitive impairment: A 6-month randomized controlled trial. *Br J Sports Med.* doi: 10.1136/bjsports-2013-093184.

The American Institute of Stress (2015). *Definitions.* Fort Worth, TX. Retrieved from www.stress.org

U.S. Department of Agriculture (2015). Washington, D.C. Retrieved from www.choosemyplate.gov

U.S. Department of Health and Human Services (2008). *Physical Activity Guidelines for Americans.* Washington, DC. Retrieved from http://www.health.gov/PAGuidelines

U.S. Department of Health and Human Services (2015). *Physical Activity*. Washington, D.C. Retrieved from www.healthypeople.gov/2020/topics-objectives/topic/physical-activity

Wolf, R., Wolf, D., Rudikoff, D., & Parish, L.C. (2010). Nutrition and water: Drinking eight glasses of water a day ensures proper skin hydration — myth or reality? *Clin Dermatol, 28,* 380-383.

POST TEST/QUIZ

1. Which word best describes the combination of physical health, mental health, and emotional/spiritual health necessary for optimal function and productivity?

2. What does the word "essential" mean as it relates to nutrition?

3. What is the only fuel source that your brain uses for energy?

4. How many minutes of exercise are recommended each week?

5. Which nutrient is considered to be the most essential and why?

6. What is the key to controlling the various distractions that attempt to pull you away from your goals?

7. How can you improve the air quality of your indoor spaces?

8. Why is it important to have a personal philosophy statement?

9. True or False: Sleeping can improve your ability to convert information into long-term memories.

10. Which component of emotional intelligence is characterized by the ability to understand and relate to what someone else is feeling?

CHAPTER 9

PATH FORWARD

By Mindy Miley

Although this trip is almost complete, there are still miles to travel. As you continue your academic journey, you will discover new roads and perhaps experience some unexpected stops. Regardless of the destination, it will always be important for you to plan wisely by setting goals, managing your time, and utilizing the tools you will need to make your journey enjoyable and unforgettable.

In order to stay motivated to continue your journey, you must believe in yourself and eliminate negative self-talk. You will also need to create distance between yourself and people or habits that make you feel badly or cause self-doubt. Positive thinking can help drown out the noisy traffic that often occurs in our mind when we begin to lose our way. To complete your academic journey you will first have to see it in your mind so each morning when you wake up and before you go to bed close your eyes and **VISUALIZE your SUCCESS**. Your vision could be an image of you crossing the stage at graduation, doing well on a speech or project, being in a dream profession, or excelling in some area that really challenges you. For example, in racing, a driver never visualizes losing or doing poorly in a race—they always visualize themselves seeing the checkered flag and taking that victory lap. Just like an athlete, you have to see it to believe it and then you can achieve it. It works the same way in academics—it's a race that requires not only planning, preparation, and hard work but also self-belief that you can reach the finish line.

In college, it is important that you are not afraid or embarrassed to ask for help. Faculty, staff, and campus support services exist because of you! The goal of faculty and the support services on campus is to help guide you toward the best path for success. However, you must take the initiative to stop along the way to use these resources and search for opportunities that will help you reach your academic and professional goals. You will find that you can maximize your experience by seeking assistance from faculty, instructors, study partners, librarians, academic advisors, tutors, counselors, peer educators, and staff in support service areas. There is incredible power in having a network of mutually supportive people to encourage you and help you achieve your goals. Building positive relationships in college and using the available resources is critical to reaching your destination of SUCCESS.

PATH FORWARD

To map out your next destination, complete this activity using the following instructions:
o It must begin with "Dear Student"
o Write your letter in a friendly, easy-to-read style
o It must be signed and dated by you
o ELABORATE: illustrate your general statements with examples whenever possible
o Utilize logical transitions from one topic to another, keep the entire letter in essay form, and try to be concise and clear in your comments
o You may wish to OUTLINE FIRST before you begin

Your letter must include a discussion of the following items:
- **INTRODUCTION:** You should introduce yourself to a future student in circumstances similar to your own, explaining briefly:
  o Where you are from
  o Why you chose this college
  o What you are planning to study or major in
  o Summarize your academic situation at the beginning of this semester and be sure to identify the challenges you faced that led to your current situation.
  o Explain two new things that you have discovered about yourself from this course experience.

- **LOCUS OF CONTROL**:
    - How would you characterize your locus of control and motivation at the beginning of the semester?
    - Explain how your locus of control or motivation/attitude has or has not changed as result of this course?

- **TIME MANAGEMENT:** Explain to next semester's student
    - What you learned about time and self-management, and
    - What time management practices you are utilizing because of this course.

- **STUDY, READING, and TEST TAKING STRATEGIES:** Tell next semester's student which FIVE study, reading, and/or test taking tips and strategies you are employing and will continue to use in the future in order to meet your academic goals.

- **DISCOVERING**: A goal of this course has been to discover the full range of educational opportunities/ resources, on-campus events, and support services. Briefly explain the most important things that you have learned about your campus in these categories:
    - Support services
    - Educational opportunities
    - Career planning
    - On-campus events

- **SELF EXPLORATION:**
    - Discuss at least two self-assessment/learning inventories that you completed this semester that has helped you the most or been the most intriguing. The inventories can be related to academic, personal, or professional success.
    - Explain how you plan to make use of this knowledge NEXT semester.

- **PERSONAL WELLNESS:**
    - Identify at least two areas related to your personal health and wellness that you have determined need to be addressed to allow you to feel better and be more productive.
    - What steps do you plan to take to address these areas?

- **STRENGTHS:**
    - Describe your strengths and how learning about these has helped you to become a more successful student and how can you use your strengths in CLASS or ACADEMICS in subsequent semesters.

- **BECOMING AN INDEPENDENT LEARNER:**
    - Discuss 3-4 ways in which you have changed or risked change over this past semester. This could be personally, academically, socially, in attitudes toward college, feelings toward your family or friends, understanding what it means to be an educated person, etc.
    - What potential obstacles stand in the way of your success? What are you going to do about them?

- **FINAL WORDS OF WISDOM:** If you could share one piece of advice with a future student, what would that advice be?

After you've written your letter, evaluate how far you have come since you started your trip. For some students it may seem that the time has passed quickly, while others may feel it took a long time to get there. Each student will have their own way to get to their final destination but the main thing is completing the journey. Student experiences may vary but it's not how you get there that's important—it's how you finish.

_____

_____

_____

_____

_____

_____

_____

_____

_____

_____

_____

_____

_____

_____

_____

_____

_____

_____

INDEX

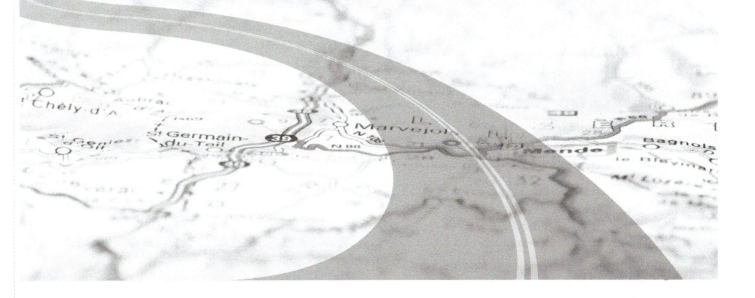

CPSIA information can be obtained
at www.ICGtesting.com
Printed in the USA
LVHW05s0858100818
586208LV00006B/18/P